KOGAN PAGE

The
Open Learning
Handbook

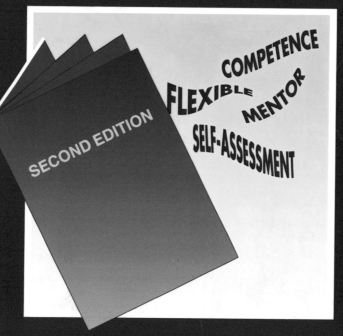

SECOND EDITION

COMPETENCE

FLEXIBLE   MENTOR

SELF-ASSESSMENT

Promoting Quality in Designing and Delivering Flexible Learning

Phil Race

UNIVERSITY OF MANCHESTER
CENTRE FOR ADULT AND HIGHER
EDUCATION

ADULT
AND HIGHER EDUCATION
LIBRARY

The
Open Learning Handbook

Promoting Quality in Designing and
Delivering Flexible Learning

SECOND EDITION

Phil Race

Kogan Page Ltd, London
Nichols Publishing Company,
New Jersey

First edition published in 1989
This second edition published in 1994

Kogan Page Limited
120 Pentonville Road
London N1 9JN

© Phil Race, 1989, 1994

Published in the United States of America by Nichols Publishing,
PO Box 331, East Brunswick, New Jersey 08816.

British Library Cataloguing in Publication Data

A CIP record for this book is available from the British Library.

ISBN 0 7494 1109 0

Library of Congress Cataloging-in-Publication Data

Race, Philip.
    The open learning handbook : promoting quality in designing and
delivering flexible learning / Phil Race.—2nd ed.
        p.   cm.
    Includes bibliographical references and index.
    ISBN 0-89397-392-0 : $39.00 (U.S.)
    1. Distance education.   2. Correspondence schools and courses.
I. Title.
LC5800.R28   1993
371.3—dc20   93-34975
                                                                    CIP

Typeset by DP Photosetting, Aylesbury, Bucks.
Printed and bound in Great Britain by
Biddles Ltd, Guildford and King's Lynn

Contents

Acknowledgements

I'm pleased to share the blame for this book – and my thanks – with very many people who have participated in my workshops on various aspects of open learning. I thank them not only for numerous ideas and suggestions, but for their arguments too.

Particular thanks are earned by John Simms, John Coffey, Trish Guerri, Maggy McNorton, John Cowan and Sally Brown. I'm also very grateful to Alex Simes and Mike Lloyd of the Information Technology Centre of the University of Glamorgan, for 'scanning-in' the original version of the book, so that I could edit and amend on-screen just about every line of it as I wished – and I did!

Without Helen Carley and Robert Jones of Kogan Page, this edition would not be here! Their professionalism and encouragement are much appreciated by this author.

Phil Race

Foreword

I've written this book for people who are involved in open learning in various ways (including authors, writers, trainers, tutors, mentors, counsellors, editors and learners too), and also for people who may be moving into the field of open learning for the first time. Since 1989 when the first edition appeared, open learning has increasingly become 'mainstreamed' in education and training, and the greatest need is no longer to find out what it is, but to find out how to use it really well.

At a time when education and training are increasingly paying attention to quality, I've made no compromises regarding quality criteria, especially ones relating to the quality of the learning experience. Most chapters contain checklists of such criteria in one form or another, and only the best open learning materials (and tutors) presently live up to these criteria.

Although this book isn't an open learning package, it adopts or includes several features of open learning. I've tried to use the sort of informal, user-friendly language which is increasingly seen as desirable in open learning materials. I've added an 'abstract' at the start of each chapter, to help you decide which chapters are most relevant to you at any given time. I've also included 'objectives' at the beginning of chapters, so you can see what you may expect to get out of them. In some chapters, I've included one or two 'self-assessment questions', and added 'responses' at the ends of these chapters, to give you an opportunity to find out what open learning *feels* like.

Why call this a 'handbook'? I've tried to cover all of the key things that people need to consider about the various aspects of open learning that I've addressed. I've also aimed to make this book self-contained and self-sufficient, and I've added an annotated bibliography at the end of the book, rather than interfere with the flow of the chapters with frequent references to the literature.

What's new about this second edition? Since 1988 I've had a great deal of additional experience in open learning, including writing, editing, tutoring, staff development, mentoring and – hardest of all – giving the odd after-dinner speech (replete learning?)! Due to this, I hope you will find the new edition more 'logical' in its approach and structure, and benefiting from the omission of one or two chapters that were somewhat tangential in its predecessor. I've tried to consolidate the main purposes of the book into ten chapters, and to develop and illustrate some arguments that I previously only hinted at. In particular, much of Chapter 1 is entirely new, looking at the one thing that should not be overlooked by anyone involved in open learning - how people actually learn.

I am grateful for all the feedback I have received about the first edition from reviewers, colleagues and friends. One of the themes of this book is 'learning from feedback' and I hope you will find that I have taken into account many valuable points raised by both critics and admirers of the original version.

Chapter 1

A Fresh Look at Learning

Abstract

In this chapter, I would like to do three main things:

- cause you to think about how you yourself learn
- give you a taste of open learning
- guide you through some questions and answers which illustrate the potential of open learning.

Most of this chapter is new to this edition of the book. I hope you find that it provides a firm basis upon which to build the ensuing discussions of designing open learning materials, and supporting learners who use them.

Objectives

When you've studied this chapter, you should be able to:

- consider a straightforward model of learning in general
- explain to other people how open learning works
- see how the skills of teachers and trainers can be directed towards helping open learners
- put open learning into perspective - as nothing new!

The need to focus on learning

Before beginning to discuss the meaning of 'open learning', I think it's timely to give you an opportunity to think about the meaning of the term 'learning' in general. Whatever sort of training we think about, or whatever sort of educational experience we consider, the one thing they all need to have in common is 'learning'. The human species is unique in its capacity for learning – that is why the species has evolved as much as it has. Human beings have been learning ever since the dawn of civilisation (and for quite some time before either of the words 'education' or 'training' were invented). Yet much that has been written about *how* we learn tends to have used language which is closer to the ways that educational psychologists think, than to the ways in which the vast majority of human beings learn. In the first part of this chapter, I would like to lead you through your own answers to three basic questions about learning, and to propose a simple yet powerful model of learning. I further propose that this model of learning can be of direct use to trainers and educators in ways which have eluded some of the more complex models of learning. The model of learning we shall explore in the next few pages of this book proves to be a very tangible basis upon which to build a strategy for developing open learning materials, and supporting learners using such materials.

At the same time as introducing my model of learning, I would like to plunge you in at the deep end regarding how open learning works. Therefore, you will shortly meet three 'self-assessment questions'. In each of these, I'd like you to jot down your own answers to the questions in the space provided, then (and only then) turn to the 'response' to each question on the page referred to.

Successful learning and demonstrable competence

Getting people to think of something they have learned successfully is a positive start to alerting them to the ways in which they learn. It does not matter what they think of as the successful learning experience of their choice – it can be work-related, or a sporting achievement, or any practical or intellectual skill. Try it for yourself – answer the pair of questions which follow now before reading on.

SELF-ASSESSMENT QUESTION 1.1

Think of something you're good at – something you know you do well. Jot it down here.

Write down a few words explaining how you became good at it.

Now please turn to page 30 and compare your answers to the questions above with the response I've given there.

How did your answers compare with the typical answers I included in my response? Did you feel when you read the response that you were able to put your own answers in perspective? As you will have seen from other people's answers to self-assessment question 1.1, relatively few people give answers such as 'by being trained' or 'by being taught' or 'by listening to experts' or 'by reading about it'. So one key to learning is 'doing'. There's nothing new about this – it's already been called 'experiential learning' for long enough – but let's stay with short words like 'doing' for the present. Next, another question.

Developing positive feelings

The matter of *feelings* has not been sufficiently explored by the developers of theories of learning. Feelings are as much about what it is to be human as any other aspect of humanity. Yet a relatively simple question yields a wealth of information about the connection between feelings and successful learning. Try it for yourself.

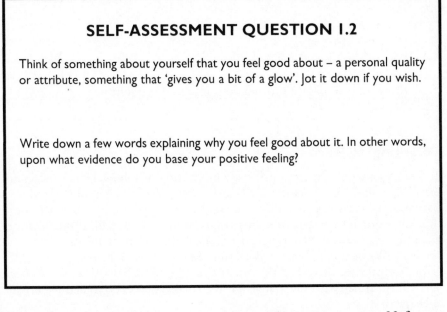

SELF-ASSESSMENT QUESTION 1.2

Think of something about yourself that you feel good about – a personal quality or attribute, something that 'gives you a bit of a glow'. Jot it down if you wish.

Write down a few words explaining why you feel good about it. In other words, upon what evidence do you base your positive feeling?

When you've jotted down your own answers, please turn to page 32 for my response.

'Doing' + 'Feedback' = successful learning?

Though these two elements are essential ingredients of successful learning, there are two further things that need to be in place. These two things are easier to tease out by asking a question about *unsuccessful learning*. Try it for yourself now, then read on.

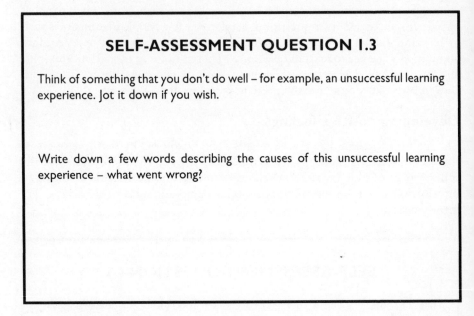

SELF-ASSESSMENT QUESTION 1.3

Think of something that you don't do well – for example, an unsuccessful learning experience. Jot it down if you wish.

Write down a few words describing the causes of this unsuccessful learning experience – what went wrong?

Now please turn to page 33 for my response to this question.

'Wanting' to learn

If there's something wrong with one's motivation, it's unlikely that successful learning will happen. However, 'motivation' is a rather 'cold' word – a psychologist's word rather than everyone's word. 'Wanting' is a much more 'human' word. Everyone knows what 'want' means. Also, 'wanting' implies more than just motivation. 'Wanting' goes right to the heart of human urges and feelings. When there's such a powerful feeling at work helping learning to happen, little wonder that the results can be spectacular. We've all been pleasantly surprised at how well people who really want to do something usually manage to do it.

If people want to learn, all is well. Unfortunately, the want is not automatically there. When subject matter gets tough, the want can evaporate quickly. In later chapters of this book, I will frequently address ways that the design of learning materials can enhance people's want to learn, and ways that tutor support and mentor support can maintain the want.

'Digesting' what one has learned

This is about making sense of the learning experience – and also making sense of feedback received from other people. Digesting is about sorting out what is important in what's been learned. Digesting is about extracting the fundamental principles from the background information. Digesting is also about discarding what's not important. It's about putting things into perspective. Digesting, above all else, is about establishing a sense of *ownership* of what has been learned. It's about far more than the nearest word the psychologists come up with – 'reflection'.

I've asked thousands of people the three questions we've looked at, and even got most of them to write their answers down. The people I've asked have covered all age ranges, different occupations and professions. It did not surprise me to discover that very different people still manage to learn in broadly similar ways. After all, learning is a *human* process – it matters little whether you're a human trainer, a human student, or a human manager.

In face-to-face training, or large-group-based education, learners are already surrounded by people who can help with the 'digesting' stage – most importantly, each other. When learners put their heads together informally to try to make sense of a difficult idea or problem, a lot of digesting occurs. In open learning, however, there may be limited opportunities for learners to use each

Wanting	– motivation
Doing	– practice – trial and error
Feedback	– other people's reactions – seeing the results
Digesting	– making sense of it – gaining ownership

Figure 1.1 *Four consecutive learning processes?*

other in this way, or even no opportunity at all. Therefore, the onus falls on the designers of open learning materials to plan-in opportunities for digesting, and also on supporters of open learning (for example tutors and mentors) to help learners digest what they are learning.

Learning cycles?

Probably the best known learning cycle is that involving the stages 'active experimentation', 'reflective observation', 'concrete experience' and 'abstract conceptualization' (see Figure 1.2). One problem I have with this cycle is that it is not too clear where it is best to start – or indeed which way round to go. Neither is it clear in which order the four steps should be connected (you will notice I've not included any arrows). Another problem I have is the words chosen for the steps in such cycles. I'm quite happy that 'active experimentation', 'reflective observation', 'concrete experience' and 'abstract conceptualization' collectively mean the same as 'wanting', 'doing', 'feedback' and 'digesting' – but try asking people to explain what the terms in the former list mean! (Asking

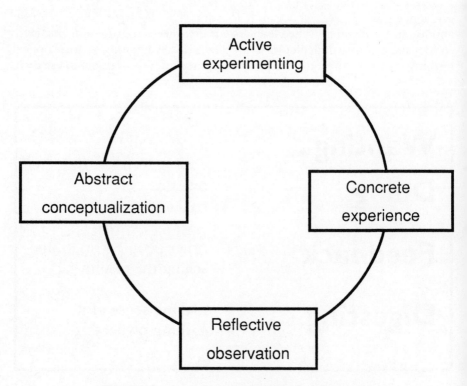

Figure 1.2   *A popular representation of a learning cycle*

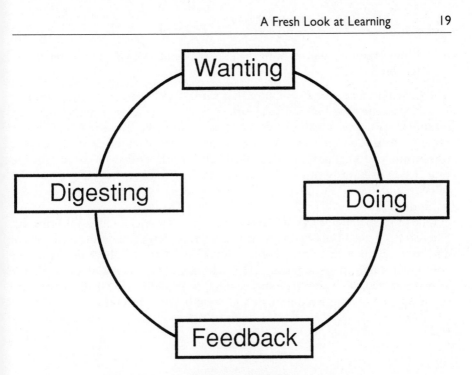

Figure 1.3 *An alternative model of learning processes*

people to define 'concrete experience' for you will produce more than one reference to sand and cement!)

In fact, I think that there are times when one needs to be in two places at once in the cycle. Also, the terminology in the cycle in Figure 1.2 may mean a lot to those who think they know what it all means, but it leaves most other people quite cold. It's tempting to try drawing a cycle with 'wanting', 'doing', 'feedback' and 'digesting' as in Figure 1.3. At least there seems to be an obvious logical order.

But are we really going round in circles?

Although I am keen to acknowledge the usefulness of thinking of learning as a combination of processes, I think that imposing a cyclic order on learning processes is - to say the least - a gross oversimplification. In fact, the more that the four processes can be made to overlap, the better. For example:

- it's important to keep on 'wanting' while 'doing'
- it's useful to be seeking 'feedback' while 'doing' as well as after 'doing'
- it's useful to be continuing to seek 'feedback' while 'digesting'
- it's useful to be continuing the 'doing' while receiving 'feedback' and while 'digesting'

■ it's important to 'digest' both the experience of 'doing' and the 'feedback' that is received.

The human brain is not a computer that works in a linear or pre-programmed way all the time. Our brains often work at various overlapping levels when, for example, solving problems or making sense of ideas. The 'wanting' stage needs to pervade throughout, so that 'doing' is wanted, 'feedback' is positively sought, opportunities for 'digesting' are seized, and so on. Perhaps a more sensible model would have 'wanting' at the heart, and 'feedback' coming from the outside, and 'doing' and 'digesting' occurring in an overlapping way as pictured in Figure 1.4.

One can also imagine this as a 'spreading ripples' model, fired by the wanting, where the bounced-back ripples from the external world constitute the feedback and continue to influence the doing. The effects of the feedback on the doing could be thought of as digesting. The main benefit of such a model is that it removes the need to think about learning as a unidirectional sequence. The model has about it both a simplicity and a complexity – in a sense mirroring the

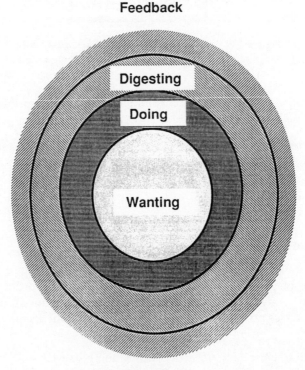

Figure 1.4 *A model of learning which caters for overlap of key processes*

simultaneous simplicity and complexity in the ways in which people actually learn.

Using the model

Probably the greatest strength of the 'wanting, doing, feedback, digesting' model of learning is that it lends itself to providing a solid foundation upon which to design educational and training programmes. If you look at any successful form of education and training, you'll find that, one way or another, all four of our ingredients of successful learning are addressed. Different situations and processes attend to each of the four in different ways.

For example, wanting is catered for by the effective face-to-face trainer or lecturer who generates enthusiasm. Wanting is catered for by carefully worded learning objectives in flexible learning materials or manuals, which capture the learners' wishes to proceed with their learning.

Learning by doing is equally at the heart of any good education or training course, and in any well-designed flexible learning package.

Feedback is provided by tutors or trainers, or by the printed responses to exercises or self-assessment questions in flexible learning materials, or by feedback responses on-screen in computer-assisted learning programmes, or simply by fellow learners giving feedback to each other.

The one that's all-too-easy to miss out is *digesting*. However, all experienced tutors and trainers know how important it is to give learners the time and space to make sense of their learning and to put it into perspective. Similarly, the best learning packages cater for the fact that learners need to be given some opportunity to practise with what they've already learned, before moving on to further learning.

Conclusions about learning in general

For far too long, learning has been considered as a special kind of human activity, with its own jargon and vocabulary. It's not! To learn is to be human. My main point is that wanting, doing, feedback and digesting are so close to the essence of being human that it's possible to keep these processes firmly in mind when designing educational courses, training programmes and learning resources – and open learning materials. It's far easier to do so than to try and work out how to engender such things as 'concrete experience', or 'abstract conceptualization' or 'reflective observation', even though such terms in fact relate to no more – and no less – than wanting, doing, feedback and digesting.

Furthermore, we need to remember that learning is done *by* people – not *to* them. In other words, it is useful to use a model of learning which learners themselves can understand. Moreover, it is important to use a model of learning which learners themselves *believe in*. The 'wanting, doing, feedback, digesting' model can easily be introduced to learners by asking them the questions I used earlier in this chapter, and they then gain a sense of ownership over the model. It often comes as a pleasant surprise and a welcome relief that there is not something mystical or magical about how people learn.

Many people returning to study later in life have hangups about things that went wrong in their previous experience of education or training, and the 'wanting, doing, feedback, digesting' model gives them renewed confidence in their own abilities to apply everyday, commonsense approaches to the business of studying.

Is open learning different?

Open learning is often talked about as though it is something quite different from 'ordinary' learning. However, by the end of this chapter, I hope you will share my view that most learning is 'open learning' – including most of the learning which accompanies traditional teaching and training, and most of the experiential learning making up life's grand tapestry. Before going any further, it's timely to look at the overlaps and differences between three of the jargon terms that come into discussions on open learning.

Open learning, distance learning, flexible learning?

The title of this book includes the words 'open learning'. However, there are two other terms that we'd better clarify first: 'distance learning' and 'flexible learning'. What's the difference between distance learning and open learning?

Open learning can certainly be done at a distance. For example, thousands of Open University students work on their own for most of the time they study, rarely attending any sort of live session. Also, thousands of correspondence students work on their own, periodically sending assignments to distant tutors for assessment and comment.

However, open learning can also happen in a crowded lecture room. Suppose the lecturer asks the class to spend a few minutes digging in some handout materials for the answers to some questions posed to the class. The class members, working on their own for a while, are essentially doing open learning for that episode: working in their own ways, at their own pace, using the handout materials as open learning resource materials – and maybe (if allowed or encouraged) using each other as resources too. Similarly, open learning can occur in laboratories, training centres, workshops – just about anywhere.

It doesn't matter whether the learner is part of a group or on his or her own, open learning can still be happening. So, we don't need to worry too much about the term 'distance learning'. The important thing is that the environment and learning materials are causing *effective* learning to happen, whether or not the learner is at a distance from the provider.

In some ways, as you will have seen from the above discussion, 'flexible learning' is the most satisfactory of the three terms. Both 'open learning' in its broadest sense, and 'distance learning' as a sub-set of open learning, involve giving learners some degree of choice and control. In other words, they introduce elements of flexibility into the learning process.

Also, there is the notion that 'open learning' may mean 'open to all comers' – the Open University in the UK is in some respects open to all. However, when it comes to advanced programmes, it just is not possible for most people to embark on a high-level open learning programme without first having succeeded on 'prerequisite' programmes. That said, the term 'open learning' is the one that's best known, and I've chosen to use it in most parts of this book, even though I'd often prefer to use the word 'flexible'!

How does open learning work?

One of the quickest ways of finding out about something new is to ask questions about it. The following pages include many of the questions which people ask about open learning. The answers I have given are intended to help to convince the questioner that open learning has much to offer, since there is no avoiding the fact that to move from traditional education or training into open learning demands much time, commitment and, often, investment.

What does 'open' mean in 'open learning'?

It means that the learners (or trainees, or students) have *choice*. They have freedom to manoeuvre. They have more control of the way they learn. There isn't as much control imposed by such people as lecturers, instructors, or teachers as in conventional training and education.

'Open' can also sometimes refer to entry criteria. Many open learning programmes attempt to dispense with strict prerequisite qualifications or experience (though of course it is necessary for learners to be aware of what they should already be able to do before starting on such a programme).

What kinds of choice and control do open learners have?

Pace
Open learners have more control over the pace they're going to work at. They can take as long as is needed to complete a chunk of studying. No more getting bored because the lecturer is going too slow. No more losing track because the lecturer is going too fast. When in open learning mode, learners have control of the rate of studying; of course, they also have the responsibility associated with making the choice a sensible one. There may still be deadlines to meet: target dates for written assignments, and even exam dates. However, the slow learner can still enjoy freedom of pace simply by putting in more hours than the rapid learner to meet the same deadlines.

Place

Open learners may be able to choose *where* to learn. Open learning can often be done at home, or in a library, or at the workplace, or just about anywhere.

Time

Open learners may be able to choose *when* to do their learning. This can mean that they learn much more effectively than they might have done at 'imposed' time slots. In face-to-face courses, how many students look bleary-eyed in morning lectures? This may be because they come to life at night rather than in the morning! With open learning, night owls can choose to do their work at night.

Processes

Open learners can also choose *how* to learn. What I mean here is that they can choose, for example, to plan out a programme of 'targets' regarding the completion of the open learning programme. The learners can choose to revise systematically. They can deliberately go back over the harder bits as many times as is needed to get them sorted out properly.

What's an open learning package?

All sorts of things can be called open learning packages. Some are entirely made up of printed material. The best print-based packages are quite different from the average textbook, however; we'll explore the differences later, in Chapter 2. Many open learning packages use audio tapes, video recordings, computer software and so on. Some open learning packages are almost entirely media-based, including interactive video programmes, and CD-I packages. So, basically, an open learning package can have many forms – the common factor is that learners can work through the package on their own.

Is open learning as good as conventional training?

This much-asked question implies that conventional training is always good. I'm sure you'd admit that much of the training you've had in the past was not perfect. When compared with 'average' training, open learning (at its best) is probably much better. (I'd better emphasize that I'm talking about *good-quality* open learning – good materials, effective learner support, and so on. Throughout this book you'll find criteria to help you sort out exactly which open learning materials may be ranked among the best.)

What's new about open learning?

Think back for a moment. Where did you do *your* learning? The *real* learning I mean. Was it done in classrooms, lecture rooms, and so on? Or was the real learning done later when you got down to it *on your own*, armed with the notes that you took from the classrooms? In fact, can't you remember learning things as exams loomed up, months after the lectures concerned, when the lectures themselves were so far back that you couldn't remember anything about them – apart from your notes? Was there any lecturer or trainer standing over you when you did most of the *real* work? Or were you working in your own way, at your own pace, *on your own*? I'm arguing that most of your real learning happened by what we're now calling open learning methods. I'd go as far as to say that open learning is the *natural* way that most learning has happened through the ages. I think it's fair to say that learning is something we do by ourselves, even when learning from other people. A good open learning package is simply something that is designed to make best use of our natural way of learning things.

So why is open learning (at its best) so good?

Well, for a start, there may be far less time wasted. For example, time – and expense – travelling to and from classrooms (or training centres) may be eliminated or reduced. More important, open learners don't have to sit there being trained in things they already know perfectly well. It's reckoned that, on average, for more than half of the time learners spend on conventional training courses, they're being taught stuff they already know! True, there are going to be some in a group who don't know it, but how sad for all the rest who already do. With an open learning package, learners can skim very quickly over stuff they already know adequately, and slow down to concentrate as soon as something new comes up. In lectures, it's not very easy to control the pace at which each member of the group learns. In fact, it's possible for some of them to learn very little! If you're teaching a group of 30, for example, at any moment you may be lucky to have two or three of them 'with you'. Others will be thinking ahead of you – and others not thinking much at all! With an open learning package, each learner is thinking at his or her own pace.

But what if parts of the learning package are irrelevant to learners' needs?

You may well decide to use an open learning package that isn't 'spot on' the subjects you want your students to learn. (This can well be preferable to taking the time to write something specially for them.) Ask yourself this, now: is each conventional lecture relevant to the needs of each individual learner?

With an open learning package, each learner can home in on those parts directly relevant to his or her present needs. The package can be retained for things which may be needed later. And if anything is totally irrelevant, the open learner can skip it. (Much less embarrassing than going to sleep during an irrelevant bit of a live session!)

So the lecturer (or trainer) is now redundant?

Far from it. A human being can do all sorts of things vital to the success of any learner. Things such as dealing with each learner's individual problems (they all have different ones). This includes things that we would like to do, but time doesn't often allow us to. The human side of open learning needs people who:

- can be counsellors, fine-tuning the learning programme to the different needs and capabilities of learners
- can select the learning modules which will be most beneficial
- can assess learners' work on the modules
- can encourage and motivate learners
- can deal with individual problems on an individual basis.

How can open learners receive human support?

Those supporting open learners can devote energy to all those things that need human skills and sensitivity. Teachers or trainers have time to do this when freed from much of the mere information-passing of conventional training. The open learning package itself does most of the routine communication of information. People supporting open learners can be available at set times for individual students who need help with their open learning studies. If Fred comes along with a problem, Fred gets the help he needs. If Fred asked his question in a lecture, everyone else has to wait as Fred's problem is dealt with. In short, as supporters of open learners we can be *resources*, rather than transmitters of information. We may in fact be very good at transmitting. But in the lecture situation, how switched on are our students as receivers? Most of the subsequent chapters in this book explore ways in which people can (1) infuse their skills into the design of open learning programmes, and (2) use their human qualities to enhance the learning experiences of open learners.

No more live sessions?

Live sessions are still very useful, but when incorporated as part of an open learning programme, they can be devoted to the things that are *best* done live. Things such as dealing with questions, developing practical skills, sharing ideas, discussing and debating, group analysis – all things where the learners *participate* rather than simply *receive*. Live sessions can be particularly useful *after* learners have done some open learning about background material; the sessions can then build on their learning. Live sessions may well be fewer, but their value to each learner will be greatly increased.

But surely there are things that can't be learned by learners on their own?

Of course there are. There are all sorts of things that are best learned through discussion and interaction. These can be dealt with in live sessions. However, in just about every subject, there are sections of theory, background material, practice exercises, and exploration that *can* be done by the learners under their own steam. So the solution is quite simple: use open learning for the things it does best, and save human resources for the things that really need human skills.

But what if learners can't retain the learning materials?

With computer-based systems, interactive video, and so on, learners won't normally be able to 'own' the learning resources. However, they will usually be able to return to the systems to brush up their knowledge. When they return, they have the advantage of revising from exactly the same resources that helped them to do their original learning, and this means that re-learning can be much quicker and more effective than might otherwise have been the case.

Is open learning cost-effective?

Certainly there *are* costs. Materials may need to be purchased, or it may be necessary to produce brand new packages if existing materials don't measure up to the learners' needs. However, there are savings as well as costs. Travelling to and from a college or training centre may be reduced, saving time as well as money. Accommodation costs may be substantially reduced – for example, when part of the study programme is done at home. For people in employment, 'time off the job' may be kept to a minimum. Moreover, experience shows that most open learners tend to take their materials home with them, even if their firm allows company time for their studies. This means that studying is being done out of paid hours – an obvious bonus for employers!

Even in conventional college courses, using open learning as an integral component of courses can bring savings: less pressure on lecture-room provision, and more availability to help people as individuals. However, cost effectiveness involves effectiveness as well as cost ! If students learn something more effectively by open learning, surely that in itself helps to justify any extra costs involved.

How well does open learning 'stick'?

Do the benefits of having studied something as an open learner continue long after the studies are completed? Indeed they do. For example, when learners are able to retain their learning materials, they have their 'trainer' right there anytime they need to brush-up or revise. The same can't be said of notes and materials acquired during conventional training. Years later, these may be quite insufficient to allow learners to recall the essence of the training sessions. Also, any good open learning module will contain a lot more detail than a set of handwritten notes. In a live lecture, it's not usually possible to write more than a few pages of notes. In the same hour or so, an open learner may be able to work through quite a lot of pages of a module. The fundamental difference is that a good open learning package *does* much of the training. Its owner therefore has the original 'trainer' on tap at any time when some revision is needed.

What does it feel like being an open learner?

Firstly, back to another question: 'What does it feel like being trained in conventional training situations?' Be honest, how many of us actually enjoy being at the receiving end of teaching? How many of us often feel a bit patronized – or even put down? A good open learning programme gives the learner the feeling 'I'm getting there under my own steam'. Open learners can enjoy much of the credit for each new skill developed. It hasn't been *given* by some other person. Things we learn under our own steam seem to stay with us for much longer than things we were taught by other people: we have a feeling of 'ownership'.

Having a good tutor can make a big difference to what it feels like being an open learner; we'll explore this in detail later in the book.

Are there no disadvantages to open learning?

Well, yes. For a start, learners studying entirely alone do miss out on the help they would have had from fellow learners in a group. For example, when Fred asks a question during a lecture, several of his colleagues may not know the answer to the question – or may not even realize that knowing the answer to that question is important. Also, learners in a group get useful information about how well (or otherwise) they are getting on by comparing their performance with that of colleagues.

Furthermore, that spark of inspiration that is generated by the best lecturers may be missed out on by the open learner. However, how many lecturers are as good as the best? Can you remember as many really inspiring teachers or lecturers as you can remember rather ordinary (to be kind!) ones?

If open learning is combined with group sessions, of course, we can have the best of both worlds. In the final chapter of this book, we'll explore in detail circumstances in conventional courses where it may be desirable to have students learning in self-study mode, rather than in lecture rooms (and even in lecture rooms too!). When using open learning it is indeed important to select the most appropriate topics for students to learn on their own. There will often be topics which really do need human teaching skills to be learned effectively.

How can I tell whether the open learning method is really working?

There's a lot of experience concerning how best to evaluate open learning programmes. You can get evidence of the learners' performance through tests and assessments, and you can monitor improvements. Even more important, however, you'll need the learners' side of things. Their views, impressions, feelings and reactions can be collected through questionnaires or interviews.

What sort of long-term future has open learning?

The term 'open learning' has been around for many years, and I hope you're now convinced that open learning has been going on for a very long time! It's not a flash in the pan or a flavour of the month. There's a strong current in the direction of greater learner-centredness. I'd go as far as to predict that the trend towards open learning will continue until the majority of post-school education and training will be using open learning methods for some (sometimes all) of the programme content.

That doesn't mean the end of live training courses but it does mean that live courses will be concentrating much more on those things where the physical presence of the trainer or lecturer is crucial. All sorts of areas not requiring such physical presence (background information, theory, practice, applications, and so on) will be studied in open learning mode, with learners enjoying the benefits of being able to work at their own pace, and at times and places which fit naturally into their daily routines (whether at home, at college, or at work).

Learners will also be enjoying the substantial benefits associated with being able to measure their own progress. A cynic said to me once: 'The advantage of open learning is that it provides privacy within which to fail!' There is some truth in this: open learners can get things wrong, then sort things out for themselves using the feedback provided in the open learning materials. This can all happen without the humiliation of having been seen to make mistakes. And it provides a good way of finding out what the likely mistakes are, and how to avoid making them in future when it really matters – perhaps in exams.

Conclusions

Open learning is indistinguishable in itself from any other effective sort of learning, though the conditions and environment *surrounding* the learning may be quite different.

Open learning can:

- accommodate directly the ways in which people learn naturally
- open up various choices and degrees of control to learners
- be based on learning materials which are learner-centred
- help learners to take credit for their learning, and develop a positive feeling of ownership of their successes
- help conserve human skills for things that really need human presence and feedback.

Responses

Near the beginning of this chapter, I included three self-assessment questions. The following pages contain my responses to these. You'll notice that the responses are a good deal longer than the questions themselves, and contain important ideas. In fact, if you skipped these questions and responses, Chapter 1 would not really make much sense to you. This is, of course, intentional. Open learning materials only work if you *do* them, rather than just *read* them.

Response to self-assessment question 1.1

It does not seem to matter at all what people choose for the thing they're good at. It also does not seem to matter what sort of people they are. I'd like you to scan through the next few pages, all of which are in their way a response to the questions you've just answered about your own learning. On the next couple of pages, I've transcribed responses I gathered from some very different groups.

The professional view?

Here is a collection of answers to the second of the above questions I obtained recently from a distinguished group of people from education, training and publishing:

- playing/practising/having some coaching
- practising – reflecting on it – talking to others and reflecting again
- trial and error, reading, observing, experimenting, remembering what worked
- reading, discussion, practice, reflection on practice/post-mortem!
- by doing it, by thinking about how to do it better, by talking to people about it, by getting feedback on how well I did it
- don't know – teasing out maths problems?
- years of action research with learners of all ages; observation, reflection on data, trying again, developing method and theory
- did it, saw whether/how it worked, reflected on why, tried again
- practice, trying different methods
- observation – how others did it; aspiration – where I wanted to get to; practice – reflect on mistakes
- by practice, by concentrating to the exclusion of other things
- by doing it not so well a lot and thinking about it.

The learners' view?

I posed the same question to a large group of students, this time getting them to write down not only how they became good at things, but also what exactly they claimed to be good at. Not surprisingly, the answers included some which make one smile.

driving	lessons, test, practice
playing the piano	practice, lessons
sex	practice, pleasure, pain
dancing	practice, lessons, experience
gardening	experience, reading about it, talking and listening to gardeners
painting	taught techniques, then practice and experimentation
essays	practice
table tennis	taught, practice, time, experience, sticking with it, endeavour
cooking	practice, necessity, interest
acting	practice, taught techniques by tutor, involving myself in pantomimes
driving	taking lessons, passing a test, driving daily, continuing to learn
driving	perseverance, determination, good teaching, bribing examiner!
embroidery	taught basics, practice and own mistakes
playing clarinet	practice, making mistakes, help from others, books, threats
swimming	starting young, practice, taking tests
swimming	practice, enjoyment
playing flute	practice, passing exams, tutoring
drinking beer	extended practice, socialising
sex	practice, pain, pleasure and struggle and hard work
tennis	practice, hard work
playing pool	practice, interest, advice, watching others
wallpapering	watching somebody qualified
mixing concrete	by trial and error after being shown how to do it
catering for 90	practice (no choice – dropped in at deep end)
making model aircraft	practice
drawing	practice, looking at mistakes, not being afraid to make mistakes, experimenting, analysing mistakes
ballet	practice, lessons, good teacher, enthusiastic at progress
talking	practice, discussions with other people
sewing	being taught, practice, enjoying doing it so practising more.

A further common thread which can be inferred from many of the students' responses above is that there is a strong connection between them developing confidence and developing competence (whatever the variety).

To sum up, in general the most frequent answers to this question are along the following lines:

- **practice**
- **doing it**
- **trial and error**
- **getting it wrong at first and learning from mistakes.**

Now please return to the main text and try the next self-assessment question.

Response to self-assessment question 1.2

My group of distinguished educationalists, trainers and publishers gave the following answers to the second of the questions above (I felt it best *not* to put them into the embarrassing position of having to write down exactly what they felt positive about):

- other people's responses
- reactions of others – feedback from others
- fun, I enjoy it, it feels good, it feels right
- because I don't feel good about not doing it; because I was told it was a good thing to do
- good feedback, seeing results, helping others to achieve things
- sense of pleasure, contentment, excitement
- other people's reactions
- compliments – reinforcement from others
- quality of finished task – concrete achievement
- feedback from others over a long period
- when I do it, I feel it 'works' – it's easy to do it well. Others confirm this for me
- people tell me they like it, positive feedback written/spoken.

A group of students gave very similar responses, as follows:

- other people tell me so
- interaction
- measuring self against others, imparting information to others
- a combination of self-assessment and assessment and observation of others
- continual feedback
- feedback, appreciation, self-confidence, recognition
- people have told me
- results, informal feedback.

Therefore, by far the most frequent answers are along the following lines:

- **reactions of other people**
- **feedback**

- **compliments**
- **seeing the results**.

All of these amount to feedback of one sort or another. Relatively few people claim that the origin of their positive feelings comes from within. Most people need to have approval from fellow human beings to develop a really positive feeling about something. Positive feelings are a crucial stepping stone along the way towards successful learning. Indeed, two of the most common things that can prevent successful learning are the absence of positive feedback or the reception of negative feedback. Criticism or disapproval can be powerful contributors to unsuccessful learning.

From the two responses so far, we've seen that *learning by doing* and *getting feedback* are vital ingredients for successful learning. However, there are still two things missing from a complete recipe for successful learning, so please return to the main text and try one more self-assessment question.

Response to self-assessment question 1.3

Here are some answers which the second of these questions yields. The causes of some unsuccessful learning experiences we had:

- no chance to practise; sheer lack of ability
- my inability to fathom technical information; no human help given
- I never learned how to 'get on the wavelength' of those who do it well
- I was warned by my father not to become competent at this activity
- did not make sense; felt bad. Could not get to grips with it. Social pressure
- insufficient commitment by teacher
- never knew when I was doing well/badly. Didn't practise sufficiently. Began too late
- the explanation was given at too rapid a speed without any acknowledgement of need to reflect and digest
- failure of confidence. Possibly I didn't really need to do it? Motivation problem?
- insufficient practice
- unrealistic explanations; damning feedback (or none)
- not allowing enough extra time to make good choices
- I didn't model it physically, kinaesthetically; I didn't get help with this.

The answers which emerge from these questions are quite complex, but the general trends hardly vary at all between very different groups in terms of age, experience, profession or vocation. It has to be said that a not infrequent response is for people to write down the name of their least favourite mathematics teacher! However, apart from this, a pattern emerges quite readily. For a start, there are usually some answers which relate to something having gone wrong with the two essentials we've already looked at. For example:

■ lack of opportunity to practise, or to learn safely from mistakes
■ 'bad' feedback – critical feedback given in a hostile or negative way.

But looking for further factors, the following are often found in people's answers:

■ no motivation
■ fear of failure
■ couldn't see why it was worth doing
■ lack of time to make sense of it
■ unable to understand it before moving on.

These boil down to two further essentials for successful learning: 'wanting' and 'digesting'. Let's next look at each of these in turn in a little more detail – please return once again to the main text on the opposite page.

Chapter 2

Designing for Open Learning

Abstract

In a way, this chapter is a summary of the whole book. It links the design of open learning materials to the model of learning proposed in Chapter 1 and then considers how the various bits and pieces which make up a good open learning package can be assembled. The main purposes of objectives, self-assessment questions, responses and assignments are mentioned, along with suggestions about how these should be linked and integrated to make up effective packages. Later chapters in this book go into more detail about each of the main components of open learning materials, but I think that it is useful to start by looking at them all together before getting into such detail.

This chapter aims to help teachers and trainers develop flexible learning materials from the resources they already use with their learners. The chapter suggests how to make an 'additionality' approach at least as effective as employing off-the-shelf flexible learning resource materials.

Objectives

After working through this chapter you should:

- see how the 'wanting, doing, feedback, digesting' model of learning is directly relevant to the task of putting together effective open learning packages
- be able to decide whether to start from scratch and write new materials, or to adopt existing materials, or to adapt existing materials
- be able to build on existing resources at your disposal, adding to them components which will allow them to work in independent-study mode
- be aware of what an open learning module isn't – ie, a textbook!

Moving from traditional towards flexible learning

It is not suggested that flexible learning should replace all traditional teaching. For many purposes, face-to-face learning situations have advantages over learning alone, and peer-group interaction is a vital part of many kinds of learning. In particular, it is possible to arrange that learners receive feedback from their peers – far more feedback than could be received from tutors or lecturers (even if not the 'expert' feedback which they need in addition). It would be sensible to examine which parts of our curriculum are best handled through each of several alternatives, including:

- large-group teaching and learning
- small-group tutorial work
- small-group unsupervised work
- individual self-study on campus
- individual self-study at a distance
- small-group self-study.

Each of these learning situations should be used for those purposes particularly suited to it. For those curriculum elements where self-study pathways or components are feasible and desirable, we can develop or acquire flexible learning resources of a suitable quality and standard.

By far the best situation in which to develop flexible learning resource materials is by being involved face-to-face with 'traditional learners'. The ultimate aim may be to produce resources which can promote learning without the presence of a tutor, but the handover of control is best done one step at a time, with thorough monitoring of each move towards learner autonomy.

A longer-term aim should be to establish distance learning pathways, built initially from those flexible learning resources which prove their worth with conventional learners.

Ten reasons for moving towards flexible learning

Why move from traditional teaching or training processes towards flexible learning? As you will probably know already, it takes a lot of work and commitment to make the switch. It's all too easy to find reasons for not making it. One of the most powerful adversaries of innovation is that basic human condition: resistance to change. Then there's fear of the unknown. Probably, however, the most popular justification for resistance to change is that it's someone else's fault anyway. 'The Institution' can't be persuaded to change its policies. If you come up against superiors or managers who need convincing of the benefits of changing policies in favour of developing open learning pathways, the following arguments may go a long way towards convincing them.

1 Increasing competition between institutions of higher education and

training means that we have to be able to *cater more flexibly* for a wide variety of learner needs and expectations.

2   With increased need for *collaboration* between providers of education and training, resource-based learning provides an easier basis for such collaboration.

3   The availability of a substantial proportion of curricula in *packaged* form significantly helps progress towards a modular structure, and allows learners increased choice.

4   Increased pressure on funding will mean we need to be able to cater both for *larger class numbers*, and for *new target groups* of part-time and distant learners.

5   As the proportion of *mature and non-traditional entry learners* increases, we need to complement traditional teaching and learning approaches by creating additional flexible learning pathways, and to replace entirely some traditional approaches disliked by mature learners.

6   With increasing use of supported self-study in secondary education, *learners' expectations* are likely to move away from being taught mostly in lectures or direct training sessions.

7   With the increased franchising of university programmes in further education colleges and in-company training departments, the availability of flexible learning resource materials provides an excellent means of ensuring that the *quality of learning* is maintained and controlled.

8   In *commerce and industry*, open and flexible learning is becoming much more attractive than traditional training (many central training departments have been restructured or even closed down).

9   It is increasingly realised that in many disciplines higher education learners are *seriously 'over-taught'*, and that this produces surface rather than deep learning, and limits learners' development of highly valued transferable skills.

10 Perhaps the most important outcome of higher education should be the development of *the ability to manage one's own learning*; flexible learning pathways develop this ability. 'Being taught' often inhibits such development.

Adopt, adapt, or start from scratch?

Having made the decision to move towards open learning provision, the next decision is about where to start. It may be possible to purchase packages that are already ideal for your learners' needs. It is more likely that there will be packages available which are not perfect, but which you can adapt, fine-tuning them to suit your learners. It is sometimes the case that there simply isn't anything suitable on the market. The following discussion may help you reach a sensible decision on how to proceed.

Does something suitable exist already?

If the 'perfect' open learning materials (perfect for your learners' needs) exist already, the most logical thing would seem to be to *adopt* them. This may mean negotiating with whoever owns the materials to get quantity discounts. If (as is often the case) there are materials which nearly meet your learners' needs, you may well be able to make up any deficiencies with tutorial support, or with things you add to the materials. Various catalogues and databases can be valuable in helping to identify and locate materials which already exist.

However, there is no substitute for getting your hands on existing materials before deciding whether they can be used as they are or whether they lend themselves to adaptation for your learners. You may need to use all the tricks you can think of to get a good look at such materials. Better still, it's worth trying a small-scale pilot before committing yourself to the purchase of large quantities of materials.

Another way of tracking down potentially relevant learning materials is through informal contacts with colleagues from other institutions. Coffee-breaks at conferences can be very profitable if used to help find people with whom you can exchange resources and information! A good checklist should be useful in helping you decide which materials may be good enough to adopt. You could use the checklist at the end of this chapter as a starting point, and refine it to tune-in better to the needs of your learners.

Have you time to start from scratch?

Writing open learning materials from scratch takes time – a lot of time! Open learning writing has often been paid for on the basis of ten hours to write up the equivalent of one hour's learning. In practice, it may take more like a hundred hours to write up one hour of learning, when preparation, piloting, editing, adjusting and so on are taken into account. If something fairly close to what is needed already exists, it can be more economical to adapt rather than start from scratch. However, you'll learn many valuable things from having a go at writing your own materials. If you really *want* to create new materials, the time issue seems to take care of itself.

Could the 'not-invented-here syndrome' affect you?

Many teachers and trainers feel a little uncomfortable working with materials written by others. We tend to prefer to work with materials where we have a sense of ownership. Even if alternative materials are better than ours, our instinct is to prefer our own, and it's only too easy for us to see all sorts of weaknesses in other people's. This can be a valid (if not entirely honourable) reason for starting from scratch and writing new flexible learning resource materials. However, the *real* reason should be the needs of our learners. If these needs are best served by writing new materials specially for them, starting from scratch is indeed justified.

What are the advantages of adapting?

Adapting existing resource materials can have many advantages, including the following:

- it can save time and expense
- you probably already own materials which can be adapted
- you can adapt materials a bit at a time
- you may be able to try out the adapted bits face-to-face with conventional classes, to gain feedback and enable improvements to be made quickly
- you *may* be able to use small pieces of published material without copyright problems or payments – but seek expert help and advice. Librarians often know a lot about copyright rules and regulations
- you'll still feel a considerable amount of 'ownership' of the materials if you've done all the fine-tuning yourself (ie, avoiding the 'not-invented-here' feeling)
- it can be much less expensive than having to purchase complete packages for each of your learners
- adapting can be excellent practice towards writing some materials from scratch in due course.

What have I got that can be used or adapted?

When you're already teaching a subject using traditional or face-to-face methods, it is not a mammoth task to translate your experience into the design of flexible learning resource materials, particularly if you are able to make the transition a little at a time. For example, it is possible to translate small elements of your normal teaching into flexible learning mode, and try them out in traditional lectures or tutorials, gaining feedback from your observations of how your learners get on with the materials, questions and feedback. Also, you can design mini-modules to give learners, covering things you decide *not* to do in face-to-face mode.

The list below is an attempt to show how well you are 'armed' for making the transition towards flexible delivery of subjects you already teach. You will have many of the following – and probably more:

- your experience of teaching – probably the most valuable resource in this list
- your knowledge of learners' problems
- your ability to help learners to find solutions to their problems
- syllabus objectives or competences you work with already
- your own handout materials:
  - usually no copyright problems
  - often already contain central material
- existing resource materials
- class exercises
  - often adaptable to make self-assessment questions

- case study details:
  - usually already the basis for learner activity, the essential part of flexible learning
- your own lecture notes:
  - these may cover most of the content your learners need, already in concise form
- textbook extracts:
  - it may be possible to obtain clearance to include small extracts without charge
  - or it may be possible to get learners to refer to books (bought or borrowed from libraries)
- manuals
  - are usually already some way towards being interactive material
  - it may be possible to use extracts without copyright difficulties
  - it may be easy to recompose extracts to avoid copyright difficulties
  - it may be possible to refer learners to 'available' manuals directly
- worksheets and assignments you already give your learners
- problems and projects you design for your learners.

What may need *adding* for flexible-learning usage?

Some or all of the principal features of the best open learning materials can be added to transform your existing materials into flexible learning resources.

User-friendly objectives

- warming up things like 'the expected learning outcome is that the student will ...' to 'by the end of ... you'll be able to ...'
- making objectives more directly relevant to learners' needs
- making them appropriate to the assessment criteria involved.

Responses to questions/tasks/activities

- not just model answers, but responses to what learners *do* when they have a go at the questions/tasks/activities
- discussion of anticipated errors/difficulties
- positive and encouraging comments for learners who have succeeded
- reassuring and encouraging comments for learners who did not succeed.

Additional questions/tasks/activities

- in self-assessment format, with responses as above.

Written study-skills help

- the sorts of help and support you'd give face-to-face learners informally.

Assessment criteria

■ to link with objectives, learning outcomes and performance standards
■ to alert learners to what counts and what could lose them credit
■ to build learners' confidence, allowing them insight into 'the rules of the game'.

Summaries/reviews/checklists

■ provide 'repeats' of crucial points, allowing learners to see what is most important
■ provide useful revision aids.

Feedback questionnaires

■ these should be short, structured, and easy-to-complete in format, but with additional space for comments from learners who want to expand on the basic questions.

Audiotape commentaries and discussions

■ relatively cheap and simple to produce
■ can make it less lonely for learners working on their own
■ can be useful for talking learners through things like textbook extracts, derivations, complex diagrams and so on
■ can also be used to help learners self-assess more complex tasks they may have done as part of their work – ie, talking them through good answers and common mistakes (can be more friendly than a long printed response).

Briefings

■ showing learners how best to use external resources such as textbooks, manuals, audiotapes, video, or practical kits.

A learning-centred approach to materials design

In Chapter 1, I developed the 'wanting, doing, feedback, digesting' model of learning, and discussed some questions and answers about the nature of open learning. The ways in which people learn in schools, colleges and training centres are very similar to the ways they learn outside them. If we're honest about it, most of the learning people do is by what we nowadays call 'open learning' processes; in other words, at their own pace, in their own way, and at times and places of their own choosing. Designing open learning materials is simply a matter of designing materials from which people can learn in their own natural ways.

Of course there's a lot more to it than just writing all the knowledge down.

Textbooks have been around for most of recorded history, and we've all experienced how easy it is to spend hours with textbooks *without* any substantial learning payoff. Learning resources need to contain much more than just information; looking at *how* people learn is the best way to determine what needs to be added.

Linking open learning to how people learn

In the discussion which follows, I would like to suggest how the design of open learning materials can be based on the 'wanting, doing, feedback, digesting' model of learning. In later chapters in this book, I will go into much more detail about the principal components of high-quality open learning materials, but first I would like to suggest some broad links.

Creating the 'want' (and responding to 'what?' and 'why?')

Motivation is a key foundation for successful learning, and in plain words motivation is about wanting. It's no use just 'wanting' vaguely, however. People need to be able to see exactly what they can learn from an open learning package, and why it will be useful to them. Several ingredients of an open learning package can be polished up so that people are attracted towards it, stimulated to begin it, and continually encouraged to persist with it.

The title

Titles can be attractive or off-putting. Which would you choose from a selection of packages with the following titles?

> *Elements of Chemical Thermodynamics IV* or *Getting to Grips with Thermodynamics?*
> *Introductory Accountancy for Turf Accountants* or *Balancing your Betting Shop Books?*

It helps, too, if the package *looks* interesting, with a stimulating and attractive cover design. After all, the title and cover also play a big part in helping people to *choose* a package in the first place.

Aims, objectives, competence statements

Not surprisingly, people want to know exactly what they will become able to do when they have worked through an open learning package. They need to be helped to *want* to achieve the objectives – and not to be frightened off by them. They need to see the relevance of the competences that the package will enable them to demonstrate (Figure 2.1).

'When you've worked through this package, you'll be able to write a good

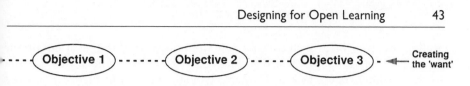

Figure 2.1   *Creating the 'want' by defining learning outcomes*

short story' is a much more attractive objective than 'The expected learning outcome of this package is that the student will be able to compose a short work of creative fiction'. (At least, I think it is!)

The introduction

I'm always telling authors of open learning materials 'You never get a second chance to make a good first impression'. It's obvious really. That first paragraph or two sets the mood in which learners proceed. The first page or so should be written with great care, preferably *after* the whole of the rest of the package has been written, so that it can point firmly towards things to come.

But I know this already . . .

No one comes to a new subject completely ignorant. Everyone knows *something* about a topic – even if it's just a series of questions they want answers to. In addition, people don't like to *feel* ignorant! Therefore, to help sustain the 'want', people need to be given credit for what they know already – it needs to be valued. One of the best ways of valuing what people already know is to give them the chance to tell you, then reply to them along the lines 'Well done, you're absolutely right'. It's perfectly possible to do this in open learning materials, by setting early exercises which most people should be able to do correctly, and responding positively to what they do. But we're overlapping already into the second and third phases of my model of learning: doing and getting feedback. (People aren't simple; all four stages overlap!)

Learning by doing – the heart of open learning

Surprising as it is to many people in the world of education (and not surprising at all to trainers), people don't learn much by sitting at the feet of the master or mistress. In addition, people don't learn much just by reading the fine words of experts. People learn by having a go themselves. They learn by doing. They learn by getting things right. They learn even more by getting things wrong, and getting feedback on what was wrong. It's particularly helpful to learn by getting things wrong *in the comfort of privacy* – one of the most powerful strengths of open learning.

When you already teach a subject face-to-face, you are likely to have a considerable collection of tasks and activities you give your learners; in other words, you are already well on your way to having one of the most important ingredients of your open learning packages. Don't forget the words you say when you introduce a task to learners. Though you may already use printed sheets for the task briefings, any additional verbal briefing is likely to play a very important part in helping learners see exactly what they are intended to do as they approach a task. With verbal briefing you have the additional advantages of tone of voice, emphasis, facial expression and body language. When translating tasks for flexible learning usage, it helps considerably if you can capture as many of these extra dimensions as possible, and wrap them up somehow in printed words.

Doing is more than just recalling

Designing an open learning package is essentially a case of designing things for learners to do, from which they can learn. Admittedly, sometimes we have to tell them a little information before they can do something useful, though usually this information can be quite minimal. Sadly, writers too often feel that they have to write down everything they know – not much help to people who learn by doing, not reading.

What can learners do?

It's not just a matter of giving learners some information, then giving them the chance to tell it back to you. Here are a few ideas, all of which can be built into tasks for learners to do: deciding, choosing, prioritizing, summarizing, arguing, defending, attacking, backing, proposing, creating, suggesting, illustrating, explaining, expressing, discussing, planning, exploring, fault-finding, criticizing, evaluating.

How soon should the doing begin?

As soon as possible! It's often possible to begin an open learning package with something interesting for learners to do – for example map out what they can already do (and can't yet do) using a checklist. When learning-by-doing is built into a package right from the start, learners quickly get the idea that the package is not just another textbook.

Self-assessment questions, activities, assignments

As soon as learners have a go at some 'learning by doing' they need to be able to find out 'Was I right?' or 'Was my choice a sensible one?' So any good learning activity will be one where it is possible to learn by doing, *and* it will also be possible to learn by getting feedback on what has been done. In short, the most important parts of any open learning package are those that learners *do*, not just read.

When planning the balance of self-assessment questions, activities and

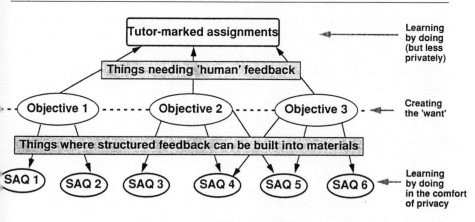

Figure 2.2 *Planning human and 'structured' feedback*

assignments, it's useful to look forward to the sort of feedback that learners are to be given. With some tasks, it is possible to give structured feedback, for example in printed responses or (with computer-based packages) in responses programmed to appear on the screen. For other tasks, feedback may need on-the-spot human judgment, and therefore such tasks are better included in tutor-marked assignments. Figure 2.2 illustrates the process of planning how learners will receive feedback, before designing self-assessment questions and tutor-marked assignments.

Getting the tasks right

When you're there in person to tell people what to do, they've got more than your words to help them work out exactly what they should be trying to do. They've got your tone of voice. There's your facial expression. There's your body language. When you're writing tasks for open learners to do, the words need to be particularly well chosen to compensate for all those other clues that aren't available to learners. The best way to get the wording of tasks right is to try out the written tasks on people in a face-to-face situation, watching how they respond to the words, and asking them whether the purposes of the tasks are clear.

Learning from feedback

I've stressed that learners need feedback to help them feel good about what they have just learned successfully – and to help them find out what they have not yet learned successfully. When learners have a go at self-assessment questions or activities, they need a lot more than mere answers. Look at it this way: all they can tell from an answer is whether they were right or not. True, that's feedback of sorts. But it's possible to give much more useful feedback if we try to *respond to what learners do*. In other words, if we ask them to make a choice, we need to be able to comment on whether they made a good choice *and* explain the justification supporting the best choice *and* explain to anyone making a different choice exactly what is wrong about it.

Feedback in print: responses – not just answers

The responses you write for self-assessment questions and activities are by far the most important ingredient of your open learning package. You should therefore give them careful attention. It's sadly all-too-easy to tell that questions and responses have been added to many open learning packages at the last minute, – almost as an afterthought. Figure 2.3 shows how feedback responses can be integrated into an open learning package.

If you think about the best-quality face-to-face teaching, some of the most important skills include:

■ explaining to learners what to do when they can't yet answer a question
■ helping learners to feel a glow when they do something correctly
■ helping learners find out exactly what went wrong when they make mistakes.

Writing open learning materials gives you the chance to package up these valuable skills so that your help is extended to learners even when you're not

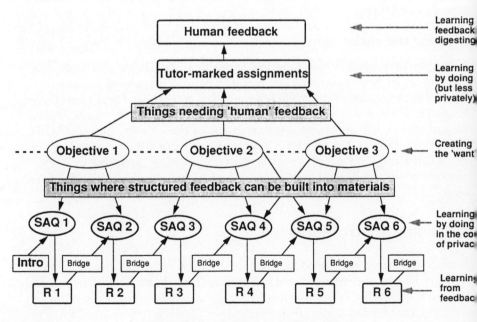

Figure 2.3 *Building in feedback responses*

there in person. The response to a good self-assessment question should enable each learner to find out two things: 'Was I right?' 'If not, why not?'

When open learning materials are scrutinized by professional open learning writers, the first thing that they turn to are the responses to self-assessment questions and activities. If these responses are working well, the package is a good one.

Structured questions are easier to respond to!

Responding to open-ended questions is possible, but usually difficult. A good response needs to cover every answer that learners may reasonably have given – and more. Structured questions involve learners making a decision such as:

■ which is the correct option?
■ which is the most sensible course of action?
■ which is the best order in a sequence?

With such questions, you can respond directly to learners who choose a 'wrong' or 'less-good' option, explaining exactly why their choice is not the best one. (In Chapter 4, we'll look at the use of structured questions in much more detail, with some examples.)

Write 'responsable' questions

Sorry about the new word that looks very much like a spelling mistake, but I've found it a useful term to use in open learning writing workshops! By 'responsable', I simply mean 'able to be responded to'. The need for feedback places limits on the sorts of questions which can be useful to learners. It's little use asking them to 'List four causes of inflation'. They may list four completely different ones from the ones we want them to list – and they may be right. Far better to ask them 'Which of the following are the four most important causes of inflation' (giving eight possibilities, say), then explaining exactly why four are more important than the others, and covering any of the possibilities they may have chosen which are not causes of inflation at all.

Praise and sympathy

When people do something well, it helps enormously to say 'well done'. There are thousands of ways of wording 'well done' messages – there's no need to be repetitious and boring about giving praise. When people get something wrong, especially working alone as open learners, they need a few well-chosen words of sympathy along with the explanations to help them on their way. The danger is that someone who gets something wrong may be thinking 'Am I the only idiot in the world who would have got this wrong?'

Phrases such as 'This was a tricky question' or 'Most people have trouble with this at first' can make all the difference.

Various sorts of feedback

Learners can benefit from printed feedback comments which respond to what they do with self-assessment questions or activities. They can also benefit from 'human' feedback – for example, that given by a tutor responding to a tutor-marked assignment. However, there are more possibilities for ensuring that learners get sufficient feedback to make them feel good about their learning.

Other people can be a vital resource. Learners can give each other feedback. Friends, supervisors, bosses, managers, employees and all sorts of other people can be a resource to learners in this respect. Learners may indeed need help in working out who to ask what for feedback.

Help learners to receive feedback well

'There is no such thing as criticism, there is just feedback.' If only it were as easy as this. However, it can make all the difference if some time can be spent with learners convincing them of the value of feedback even when it is 'negative'. Simply helping them to receive critical comment as 'criticism of something I did' rather than 'criticism of me' is a major step.

Summaries and reviews

These can be a big help in the 'digesting' stage of learning. Summaries and reviews help learners to decide what they need to retain. It can even be useful to read the summary or review *before* starting a topic as a way of finding out what it's really going to be about (especially if the objectives aren't clearly spelled out). Sadly, many open learning materials are skimpy on summaries or reviews. However, it's relatively easy – and very useful – to add-on summaries and reviews, for example by writing study-guide material to help learners to navigate an existing open learning resource.

How can a package be put together efficiently?

Turning your existing resources into an open learning package can be done more easily than you might have imagined. It's best to get the various separate components of your package into good working order, trying them out with groups of your learners whenever you can. Then gradually build the components together into a draft package and see how your learners cope with it.

At first, the task of putting together an open learning package may seem formidable, especially if you want to equal the best published packages. However, Rome wasn't built in a day, and the best open learning materials were created gradually, step by step, with a great deal of piloting at each stage. Most of these steps are simple extensions of things you do in your day-to-day work with your learners. The following sequence can save much time and trouble.

1   Design *self-assessment questions* and *activities* for your open learners based on the class-work exercises you presently use, and the assignments and projects you set your existing learners, linking these to the syllabus *objectives* or *competences* or *learning outcomes* in the same way as you already do. Adjust the wording of all these components as you go, so they becomes as straightforward and clear as possible, so that learners don't need you to explain what the words mean.

2   Write *responses* to each self-assessment question and activity. Base these responses on the way you deal with your live learners. Write in the explanations you give them when they make mistakes. Keep striving to make the questions and responses as self-explanatory as you can so that you don't need to be present in person. Try out each draft with your live learners and observe any difficulties, adjusting questions and responses as necessary.

3   Start turning your notes and handouts into short sections of text. Make these sections bridge the gaps between the *response* to one question and the next question. Each chunk of text therefore has a distinct function – to lead up to the next learner activity.

4   When there are questions or activities which really do need a human response rather than a pre-prepared one, turn the questions into *tutor-marked assignments*, and build these in to your package.

5   Go through the bits and pieces of your package, adding *summaries* or *reviews* at key points. Make such additions every time your learners may need reinforcement of principal ideas and concepts.

6   Now that your package is nearing a 'working' form, go through it again adding *short introductions* or '*lead-in*' paragraphs, preparing your learners for what is to come in each part. It's far easier to write well-tuned introductions when you've already written the parts you're leading up to. These parts are what I have referred to as 'bridges' in the strategy flowchart in Figure 2.4.

As you can see from the sequence in Figure 2.4, writing an open learning package is not done in the same way as writing a textbook. It's not a matter of writing page 1 and working through in a linear sequence.

Open learning packages are designed around the *learning* that learners will gain from them. This takes the emphasis away from the text itself, and means you don't need to try to write everything you know about the subject. Only write the things your learners *need* to gain.

It's often advisable to start working on the middle of your package, then work outwards in both directions. Writing the very beginning is one of the most crucial tasks and is much easier to do if you've already written later parts of the package. You know then exactly what you're introducing.

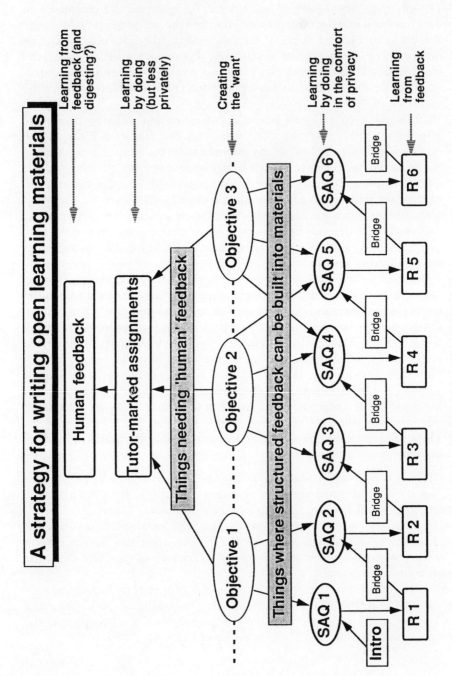

Figure 2.4   *The complete picture*

Helping learners use flexible learning materials

The following suggestions can help learners adjust their approach to using flexible or open learning materials. I suggest that you fine-tune and develop your own advice to your learners, starting from the list below, by adding-in comments relating to the particular style and format of the materials they will be using.

1   Check whether there are things you should already be able to do before you start working through the open learning materials. Information such as 'prerequisites' is often given at the start. It's also useful to look ahead at the self-assessment questions and activities, to see whether you think you can already do many of them. After all, there's no point starting at the beginning of the package if you can already do everything in sections 1 and 2.

2   If the material gives *objectives* or intended learning outcomes in one way or another, pay particular attention to these and keep returning to see how well you are getting on towards mastering them. Objectives are usually phrased along the lines 'When you've completed this package, you should be able to . . .'. Alternatively, you may find statements of 'competence' and 'performance criteria'. Again, these are your targets; keeping your eye on them pays dividends.

3   Most open learning materials are 'active' and contain things for you to do as you work through them. These active-parts are sometimes called *self-assessment questions* or *activities*. However tempted you are to skip these and read on, don't! Even if you think you know the answer, jot it down, *then* compare what you did with the answer or response given in the material.

4   When you get a question right, be pleased with yourself. When you get one wrong, be even more pleased – you've found out something useful. Find out exactly *why* you didn't get the right answer, and remember this for next time. Learning by getting things wrong at first is a highly productive way of learning, and with open learning materials, no one else sees.

5   When you come to a bit that has you stumped, don't struggle with it for ages. Skim ahead – the next bit may be straightforward. Make a note of exactly what you don't understand about the bit that stumped you, and plan to find out from someone how to deal with that bit. It's probably quite simple when you've got someone who can explain it to you, even though you may never have worked it out on your own.

6   Open learning materials often contain a great deal of information. Don't try to learn it all as you proceed. Make decisions about what you *need* to learn, as opposed to the things you merely need to understand as you read them. It's very useful to work with fellow learners for this if you've got the chance – you'll all have slightly different views about exactly what is important and what isn't, and the truth will be closer to the 'average' view than to one person's view.

7   If you've been given your own copy of the open learning material, make it *belong* to you by writing your own comments and notes all over it (as well as by writing in the answers to questions and activities). You'll often remember the things you added to the material – a useful way of boosting what you remember about the topics involved. Also, use highlighter pens to remind you of the really important bits.

8   Keep looking back. Remind yourself of the things you've already done. The more often these things have been through your mind the more firmly you'll understand them. Don't allow things you've mastered to slip away from you. Even a few minutes looking back can be a very useful investment. Once you've learned things, it takes very little time to *remind* you of what you became able to do with them.

9   Keep glancing ahead to see what's coming next. You'll often understand *why* you're doing something only when you see where it's leading towards. Headings are a very useful guide to how the learning material is going to unfold, and it only takes a minute or two to scan ahead and see how the material is going to develop from where you are at a given time.

10 Have *another* go at all the self-assessment questions and activities – again and again where they are difficult. Your ability to do something difficult depends more on how often you've tried doing it than on how thoroughly you did it once. If you're heading towards formal assessment such as exams, you will be required to answer questions very similar to the self-assessment ones, so get plenty of practice in.

Helping open learners to use other resource materials

'Briefings' represent one area of support and advice that is normally handled quite informally in face-to-face sessions. Learners at such sessions have the extra advantages of tone of voice, and facial expression, helping them find out more about exactly what they're intended to do with the textbooks and literature references they're given. The same level of support needs to be put into print if learners studying by flexible learning pathways are to derive the same amount of benefit from briefings to resource materials. The following suggestions give some ways of ensuring that printed briefings serve learners effectively.

■   *Keep them short and specific.* It is better to have briefings to short extracts than to whole books or chapters. For example, 'Now work through Sections 2.3 and 2.5' is better than 'Now read Chapter 2'.

■   *Make briefings active.* Don't just ask learners to read things, give them things to do *while* they read them – or even before reading things (not just after they've read them).

- *Include 'commentary' elements in briefings.* For example, 'Chapter 3 gives a good overview of...', 'Watch out particularly for the way ... is discussed', 'Don't worry about... at this stage, you don't need to know the sort of detail that you'll see in Section 3.5'.
- *Include 'signposting' in briefings.* For example, 'In Section 4.8 we've already seen why ... happens. In Section 4.9 you'll find out what happens when ..., which is useful when you need to work out how to ...'.
- *Plant questions in learners' minds.* When learners have already got some questions in mind before reading something, they have a subconscious 'thirst' for the answers to the questions. This means that when they come across the 'answers' as they read, those parts are more memorable to them. This makes reading far more efficient.

    For example, 'As you study Section 6, try to find answers to the following three questions:

    Why does...?
    How could...?
    When might you find...?'
- *Include 'steering' in briefings.* For example, 'You don't need to spend much time on Section 7 unless you *want* to', 'The heart of the matter is explained very well near the end of Section 5.7', 'Aim to spend about half an hour simply getting the feel of Chapter 4 before having a go at the next set of self-assessment questions'.
- *Help learners to find out for themselves which parts they need to concentrate on.* This can be done by using self-assessment questions to measure how much different learners already know about a topic, and using the responses to route each learner accordingly. For example:

Before you move on to Chapter 3 of the textbook, have a go at SAQ 23 below.
SAQ 23
Before studying 'waldefaction' in Jones and Smith, have a go at the following six questions to see if you already know something about it (don't worry if not – it's all in Jones and Smith!)

-
-
-
-
-
-

Response to SAQ 23 (out of sight of the question)

■   *(correct answers)*
■
■
■
■
■

If you got all of these right, well done, and you only need to look at Sections 3.7 and 3.9 in Chapter 3; you already know all you need to from the other sections.

If your only mistake was to . . . , you'll find out what to do about it at the beginning of Section 3.2. The only other parts of Chapter 3 you should give particular attention are Sections 3.7 and 3.9 . . .

If you didn't get much of this SAQ right, don't worry, it's all covered in Chapter 3. As you work through this chapter, take particular note of Sections 3.2 and 3.4 – these contain what you need to know to do questions like SAQ 23 . . .'.

Writing study guides

Some flexible learning programmes hardly contain any subject matter in the normal sense of the term, but are written to guide learners through an existing resource such as a 'reader', or through a selection of resource materials. The Open University, for example, often adopts key reference books as the major source of information in a course.

The open learning packages then become interactive guides to the books. All that I said earlier about briefings continues to apply to this sort of guidance. It remains particularly important that when learners have completed a task or activity based on the reference material, the study guide provides them with true responses to what they have been doing.

The 'books plus study guide' format solves several problems. Copyright is taken care of, as learners purchase (or are loaned) the original source material. Economies of scale are possible, as mass-produced books tend to be less expensive than open learning modules produced in runs of only hundreds. Any study guide is much slimmer than the corresponding material would have been if it had been put together in fully interactive open learning style.

The study guide format depends, of course, on the availability of the resources to be used. If a textbook goes out of print, or becomes dated and superseded by new work, the study guide too will at once be redundant. However, it remains less expensive to revise or renew a 'slim' study guide than to redesign a full open learning module.

Key elements of a study guide

- intended learning outcomes (there probably aren't any in the accompanying textbook)
- detailed briefings, showing exactly what to look for in the textbook, and where to search for it
- self-assessment questions and responses, to allow 'learning-by-doing' and feedback – exactly as in a good open learning package
- tutor-marked assignments, if tutor support is available
- perspective-setting material (to help 'digesting'), so that learners can approach the source materials in a realistic way and strike a sensible balance in the emphasis they place on ideas and concepts
- explanatory bits to help learners make sense of anything that may be handled less than adequately in the source material.

Some general tips for writers

- Avoid sitting thinking about writing – write! Set yourself stage deadlines; better still, let other people know about your deadlines. Work on small manageable jobs – don't try to work on the whole package at once.
- Show your writing to other people (learners, colleagues, friends) long before it's 'ready'. Critical feedback on an early draft is easier to swallow than criticism of your completed masterpiece.
- Keep the tone relatively informal. Use 'you' for your learners, 'I' as the author. As far as you can, try to make the printed page 'talk' to your learners in the same way as you would have talked yourself – particularly when explaining things.
- Remind yourself now and then that you're not writing a major treatise, or a paper for an esteemed journal in your field. You're writing for your learners. Don't stand on your professional dignity in your writing.
- Use plenty of *white space*. Leave room for your learners to write in their answers to your questions, and their own notes and comments. Your learners will develop an important sense of ownership of the materials as they write all over them.
- Use short words rather than long words where possible. Get your meaning across as directly as you can (there's no tone of voice or facial expression to help your open learners).
- Use short, simple sentences rather than long, complex ones. Aim to get your meaning across on the first reading of each sentence. Be particularly careful when setting questions and tasks. Make sure that learners will know exactly what they are intended to do with each task.
- Include headings and sub-headings so that learners can see at a glance what each page is doing. If your learners can see where they're going, and where they've been, their journey through your open learning package is more likely to be successful.

■ Include illustrations wherever they help learners to understand things. Illustrations also help to keep learners going – a page with something visual on it looks more enticing than a solid page of text.

Piloting – the best guarantee of quality

You may have seen many open learning materials which *look* marvellous – but don't work! These are packages which were 'glossed-up' and published long before they were ready. The more feedback you can get about how your package works, the better you can make your final version. The best open learning packages owe as much to the experiences of the learners who tested them out as to the skills of the authors.

You don't have to wait until you've got a finished product before starting to gather feedback. You can try out each small part as you compose it. For example, with the help of your learners, you can test your self-assessment questions and responses. You can try out your tutor-marked assignments. You can change things every time you find a problem.

When eventually you have a first draft of your package assembled, it's useful to try this out on some learners (and on some colleagues), deliberately seeking detailed feedback by providing questionnaires and talking to your piloteers.

Among other things, make sure you ask questions such as:

■ What is the best thing about the package?
■ What do you like least about the package?
■ What do you think is the hardest part of the package?
■ What do you think of the tone and style of the package?
■ How clear are the objectives of the package?
■ How useful are the self-assessment questions and activities?
■ How helpful are the responses to the self-assessment questions and activities?
■ Do you think there are sufficient illustrations?
■ How useful are the summaries and reviews?
■ How long do you think the package takes to work through?
■ Suggest some changes which can improve the package.

Open learning versus traditional textbooks

In this chapter, we've explored what makes open learning tick, and how the various bits and pieces can be assembled as effectively and efficiently as possible. In later chapters, I'll discuss in greater depth the design of the individual components on which open learning packages are based. You probably already realize that it takes a good deal more time, skill, and patience to put together an effective open learning package than it does to write a simple textbook. As a result, open learning packages tend to cost quite a lot more than textbooks. Another reason for this is the fact that popular textbooks are often printed in extended runs of several thousand, bringing down the unit cost. Open learning packages are more often produced for somewhat specialized target groups and the print runs are normally much smaller, taking the unit cost up even further.

Because plain textbooks tend to be cheaper, it is worth looking at exactly what the added value of an open learning package may be. In the commentary below, I'm deliberately going to compare an 'excellent' open learning package with a 'bad, old' textbook! May I confess at once that the comparison is biased. I'm well aware that many textbooks are not at all like the 'bad, old' ones I refer to. In fact, many successful modern textbooks use several of the features you'll find in the best open learning materials. However, even with these reservations, the worst thing that can be said about some open learning material is that it is 'textbookish'! Therefore, when selecting and evaluating open learning materials, criteria such as those mentioned in the comparison below will be useful.

Before launching into my biased comparison, however, I'd like to air a worry about the 'textbook society' in general. People who write textbooks tend to have thrived on learning from print. People who read textbooks and learn from them are, in a way, highly developed 'open learners' – after all, they use textbooks in their own way, at their own pace, at places of their own choosing, and so on. The textbook is a resource which is used in an open learning manner. However, many people who need and want to increase their knowledge and skills are *not* the sort of people who thrive on learning from textbooks. These people may benefit from help in structuring what they do with printed resource materials. They may need to have definite things to help them 'learn by doing'. They may particularly need the benefit of receiving feedback on what they do as they learn. They may need their 'want to learn' to be continually amplified and reinforced. They may need help in 'digesting' things as they master them. All of these things are implicit in the design of open learning materials.

Now for the biased comparison!

Content

Open learning materials are interaction-centred; it's what learners *do* that really matters. Learning happens by 'having a go', then getting feedback.
Textbooks tend to be content-centred: the content is often the be-all and end-all.

Motivation (the 'want to learn')

Open learning materials are written so as to get learners interested and involved. Learners may already be highly motivated, or alternatively may have been instructed to do the learning concerned by a superior at work.
Textbooks often assume (perhaps wrongly) that readers are already interested. How many textbooks spend much of their lives unopened on shelves?

Self-esteem

Open learning materials (especially the best ones) cultivate and develop the self-esteem of learners. Learners are given the framework within which to think things out for themselves; they then have greater 'ownership' of the skills and knowledge they develop.

The average **textbook** merely presents its reader with information; readers don't benefit from a feeling of 'ownership' of their progress.

Relevance

Most **open learning materials** are purpose-built to be wholly relevant to the needs of a target group of learners.

Many **textbooks** tend to concentrate on the things the authors wish to present. Only certain sections of the average textbook are directly relevant to any individual learner. Students are often lacking in the essential skill of being able to track down the relevant parts of textbooks. Few realize how useful contents pages and index sections can be for this purpose.

Ego trips

A **good open learning module** gives the successful learner a confidence boost. Learners feel they can take much of the credit for their newly acquired skills and knowledge. Much of the learning has occurred in an experiential way, through having a go at self-assessment questions or assignments, then benefiting from the feedback provided in the learning materials. When learners get things wrong, their mistakes are made in private, not in public. Don't we all learn much from our mistakes?

It can often be said of **textbooks** that it is the author who has taken the ego trip.

Structure

Open learning materials are structured to meet the learners' needs. The author's original drafts are often changed quite drastically during editing and after piloting, so that learners are as well served as possible.

Most **textbooks** have structures which were largely provided by the authors. Few textbooks are piloted in the same way as good open learning modules are; nor are they adjusted radically to meet learners' needs.

Questions and answers

Open learning materials include many questions, particularly self-assessment questions. The best open learning materials don't just have answers to such questions, they have *responses*. A response is much better than a mere answer. Responses help learners find out (in private) exactly why they made particular mistakes, for example. We'll explore self-assessment in detail in Chapter 4.

Many **textbooks** have questions and answers, but relatively few readers actually attempt the questions. It's usually only the really conscientious learners who attempt textbook questions systematically – and they probably need them least. There may be little help if they don't manage to get the right answer first time.

Assumptions and errors

When an **open learner** makes a false assumption or error, the good open learning module will quickly show what this was, and why it happened. Self-assessment questions are designed to show learners whether they are making any such assumptions or errors.

With **textbooks**, it may be only too easy to press on with false assumptions, leading to flawed learning.

Objectives

Open learning materials use objectives, or competence descriptors, or statements of learning outcomes, to help learners see exactly what they're supposed to become able to do. Such devices also provide learners with the means to test how they're getting on. We'll explore some of the finer points regarding writing these devices in Chapter 3.

Textbooks sometimes give objectives or descriptors of intended outcomes, but they're rarely turned into an active and useful part of the way the reader is directed to handle the information presented.

Tone and style

Most **open learning materials** use 'friendly' language. The learner becomes 'you'. The author is 'I'. The learner feels part of what is going on. We'll look at tone and style aspects in detail in Chapter 5.

Textbooks are usually written in the third-person passive style. The tone is objective, but remote and impersonal – and often boring.

White space

Many print-based **open learning modules** leave white space for learners to write in. Learners may also be ticking boxes, adding to diagrams, filling in numbers in tables, and so on. Computer-based open learning materials often allow learners to enter things via the keyboard. All this adds to the involvement of the learners (even working on their own). The learning materials soon begin to 'belong' to the learners much more, due to all the things they write or draw into them.

Textbooks often cram every available space on each page with information – text, figures, tables and so on. Have you noticed how, in textbooks, a major heading often appears well down a 'right-hand' page, rather than at the top of the next page? (I hope this isn't the case with the present book!)

Active visuals

In **open learning materials**, when diagrams, graphs, tables, charts and so on are used, they are used *actively*. Learners are asked to do things with them. Learners use them, add to them, interpret them, pick out trends and so on.

In **textbooks**, diagrams, graphs, tables, charts and so on are simply there. The reader may or may not take much notice of them.

Visuals: expectations?

In **open learning materials**, learners will usually be told exactly what the intention is regarding things like diagrams, graphs, tables, charts and so on. Learners *need* to know whether they have to be able to reproduce the information concerned, or simply pick out trends, or recognize it next time and so on.

Textbooks rarely help the reader regarding whether the visual information is to be learned, or understood, or merely noted in passing. By default, most just gets noted in passing.

Manageable chunks

Good **open learning materials** take into account the fact that concentration spans are limited. Material is broken down into manageable sections, each with a start, a middle and an end.

Textbooks tend to present large amounts of material at a time, the author continuing until he or she has said all that can be said about each topic.

Study skills advice

In the best **open learning materials**, there are frequent tips for learners, regarding how best to get to grips with the various ideas, concepts and information.

With many (but not all) **textbooks**, how the reader learns is not usually seen as the author's concern. Readers are left to their own resources regarding the development of their study skills.

Summaries and reviews

With **open learning materials**, each chunk ends with some sort of summary or review. This is vital to help learners in the 'digesting' stage of their learning. The review may well be made an active event, for example by presenting learners with a checklist so that they can test out how well they've got on with the material.

Textbooks often have summaries or reviews, but usually only at the end of rather long instalments of material. Textbook review sections are rarely turned into an activity for readers.

How am I doing?

Open learning materials try to answer this question continuously. Self-assessment questions and responses help to do this, so do objectives, reviews and summaries. All of these help learners get the feedback they need. The learner is not left long in doubt.

Most **textbooks** give little help to the reader who wants to know 'how am I doing?'

Feedback and modification

It is usual for **open learning materials** to be piloted quite extensively. Feedback is gathered from the learners themselves via questionnaires, interviews and so on. Modifications are made whenever snags are encountered.

The only feedback many a **textbook** author gets is from academic peers – reviewers or referees. The average reader's views may not easily get back to the author. The exception is when a good textbook gets into third, fourth, fifth editions. But how many textbooks are that good?

Human back-up

It is usual to have some form of tutorial support for **open learners**. This may take place in distance mode, face-to-face mode, or both. Open learners who have difficulties may depend on this support. Human support can even turn quite poor open learning materials into successful learning resources.

There may not be such support for the **textbook reader** who has difficulties.

Finally, may I once again point out that the purpose of the above comparison is to provide food for thought about some of the features which make open learning materials different – and to offer some justification for the higher costs of open learning materials in general. That said, there will always be room for textbooks too.

Quality checklist for flexible learning resources

To conclude this chapter, I have attempted to draw together all the strands into one manageable chunk – a checklist of things to look for when judging the quality of an open learning package. The checklist which follows is quite powerful! If all the answers are 'yes' or 'very well indeed', you're looking at an exemplary piece of open learning material. However, even when some of the criteria below are not met, all is not lost. In fact, it's very useful to identify exactly which criteria aren't met by a particular piece of flexible learning material; you are then in a position to compensate for whatever's lacking. It often only takes a few extra words or lines to plug a gap in some material, or to help learners to make better use of it.

If you are writing your own material, you should find this checklist a useful self-editing resource. I've clustered the 30 checklist questions under sub-headings representing the main elements of flexible learning materials identified earlier in this chapter.

Objectives or statements of intended learning outcomes

1   Is there a clear indication of any prerequisite knowledge or skills?
2   Are the objectives stated clearly and unambiguously?
3   Are the objectives presented in a friendly way? (That is to say, *not* 'the expected learning outcomes of this module are that the learner will...'!)
4   Do the objectives avoid jargon which may not be known to learners before starting the material?

Structure and layout

5   Is the material visually attractive?
6   Is there sufficient white space for learners to write notes, answer questions, do calculations and so on?
7   Is it easy for learners to find their way backwards and forwards? (This is sometimes called 'signposting' and includes good use of headings.)

Self-assessment questions and activities

8   Are there plenty of them? (Remember that flexible learning, like any other learning, is largely dependent on 'learning by doing'.)
9   Are the tasks set by the questions clear?
10   Are the questions and tasks inviting? (Is it clear to learners that it's valuable for them to have a go rather than skip?)
11   Is there enough space for learners to write their answers?
12   Collectively, do the self-assessment questions and activities test learners' achievement of the objectives?

Responses to self-assessment questions and activities

13   Are they really *responses to what the learner has done* (rather than just answers to the questions)?
14   Do the responses meet the learners' need to find out:
'Was I right?'
'If not, *why* not?'
15   Do the responses include (non-patronizing) encouragement or praise for learners who got them right?
16   Do the responses include something that will prevent learners who got it wrong from feeling like complete idiots?

Introductions, summaries and reviews

17 Is each part introduced in an interesting, stimulating way?
18 Do the introductions alert learners to the way the materials are designed to work?
19 Is there a clear and useful summary/review?
20 Does it provide a useful way to revise the material quickly?

The text itself

21 Is it readable and unambiguous?
22 Is it relevant? (For example, does it keep to the objectives as stated?)
23 Is it 'involving' where possible? (There should be plenty of use of 'you' for the learner, 'I' for the author, 'we' for the learner and author together.)

Diagrams, charts, tables, graphs and so on

24 Is each as self-explanatory as possible?
25 Does the learner know what to do with each? (Are they to learn it, note it in passing, pick out the trend, or even nothing at all?)
26 'A sketch can be more useful than a thousand words': is the material sufficiently illustrated?

Some general points

27 Is the material broken into manageable chunks?
28 Does the material avoid any sudden jumps in level?
29 Does the material ensure that the average learner will achieve the objectives?
30 Will the average learner *enjoy* using the material?

Conclusions

When designing open learning materials, whether print-based, computer-based, or multimedia packages, what matters is 'how it works'. This is much more important than the content of the materials. The keys to quality are the elements of the materials which mesh with the ways that people actually learn. The best materials will create the *want* to learn, provide abundant opportunities to *learn by doing*, provide a great deal of useful *feedback* to learners, and take account of the fact that learning does not happen instantly, but needs time for *digestion*.

If you're already working face-to-face with learners, you have several advantages when it comes to gradually turning parts of what you do into flexible learning resources:

- you know your learners – one of your target audiences
- you can try things out and get quick feedback on whether they work or not

■ you can turn existing class-exercises and homework questions into self-assessment questions and activities

■ you can turn the feedback you would give orally or in comments on marked work into printed responses to self-assessment questions and activities

■ you can transform your own notes into the textual parts of flexible learning materials

■ you can continue to use face-to-face sessions for the things that are difficult to wrap up in print.

In this chapter, I've been concentrating on those components of learning packages which can help open learners to learn productively, using their natural ways of learning. However, even the best open learning package can work even better if it is well supported from outside – for example by tutors or mentors. Human helpers can be even more responsive than print when it comes to providing learners with feedback on what they have done. Moreover, human helpers can help maintain open learners' motivation – in other words, keep them *wanting* to learn. We will look at human support in much more detail later.

Chapter 3

Learning Outcomes – Showing Open Learners Where They're Heading

Aims

This chapter aims to help you explore the role of expressed learning outcomes in open learning materials. I would also like to help you ensure that statements of learning outcomes in material you write are positively *useful* to your learners, rather than simply adorning the first page or the inner front cover. If you're adapting or using materials which already have stated learning outcomes, you may find that you can improve them considerably by making them play a more important part in the structure of the materials.

Objectives

When you've practised with the ideas in this chapter, you should be able to:

- distinguish between aims and specific learning outcomes such as objectives
- write clear, precise learning outcomes
- explain the relationships between a competence statement, performance criteria and range statements
- formulate learning outcomes which are directly helpful to learners, open learners in particular
- use expressed learning outcomes to play a major role in open learning materials.

Different ways of expressing learning outcomes

When I wrote the first edition of this book, the most common way of expressing intended learning outcomes was in terms of behavioural objectives. I was then somewhat critical of the fussy way that was often used to divide objectives into various domains and hierarchies, and my chapter on objectives concentrated on ways of making them useful directly to learners themselves.

Since then, it has become common to express learning outcomes in the form of *competences* which learners should be able to demonstrate as proof of success in their learning. Here too, there is the danger that competence statements can become over-complex and elaborate, with *performance criteria* assigned to each competence, and *range statements* showing within which limits each element of performance should lie.

The intention behind all these ways of providing details of intended learning outcomes is positive – to help learners to see exactly where they're heading, and what they are trying to become able to do. I hope that this chapter alerts you to the potential that can be realized by spending time and energy adjusting the wording of intended learning outcomes, as well as to the danger that can accompany efforts to try to make expressions of learning outcomes totally rigorous.

Syllabus or learning package?

Syllabus content is now widely expressed in terms of intended learning outcomes, both in education and training. The ways such outcomes are expressed varies from one discipline to another, and from one level to another. In the UK, vocational syllabus content (for example in programmes of study linked to National Vocational Qualifications (NVQs)) are normally expressed in terms of elements of competence (showing *what* learners are intended to become able to achieve), each of which is amplified by performance criteria (usually showing *how* learners are intended to become able to demonstrate each competence), and range statements (describing the intended minimum and maximum levels of competence).

There still remain many syllabuses written in terms of behavioural objectives, simply giving details of what learners are intended to become able to do, without much detail of the levels of performance to be developed. And, of course, there are still 'aims'. Let us start with these.

What is an 'aim'?

I've got to admit to some cynicism regarding aims! You'll no doubt have seen aims adorning many an objectives-based syllabus. Such aims are usually followed by lists of sharper learning outcomes. The learning outcomes are needed to spell out exactly what the aim means. I sometimes think that the people who write aims in such a syllabus have the following definition in mind:

> An aim is something you write near the top of a syllabus, which no one can prove your learners haven't achieved.

So what *is* an aim? I'd settle for either or both of two descriptions:

- a broad statement of intent
- a 'flavour statement', giving some ideas of what's to come.

It's not really possible to return to an aim and use it to test out whether the learning has been successful. We need sharper tools for this purpose. Have a look again at the aims I started this chapter with. Do you notice that they're really quite broad, and they don't give you much help about exactly what will be involved in achieving them?

What is an 'objective'?

It's a sharper, more precise statement of intent. An objective (in learning materials) is usually a statement along the following lines:

When you've completed this module, you should be able to:

- sketch a grommit
- list the three main requirements for an effective grommit
- explain why grommits can't be used alongside an electric gubbins
- speculate on the effects of using copper grommits instead of steel ones.

In a syllabus, to be used by teachers or trainers, the words which lead up to each objective are not of great significance – the important parts are the objectives themselves. In a learning package, however, how the learning outcomes are presented makes a considerable difference to how they are received by open learners.

There are many ways of introducing the things that the learners should expect to achieve. Alternative introductory phrases include:

- When you've worked through this section, you'll be able to . . .
- When you've completed this package, you'll be able to answer each of the following questions . . .

However, I've often seen materials which begin with a statement like:

The expected learning outcome of this module is that the student will be able to . . .

This sort of objective-writing is obviously *not* addressed to learners themselves; it's more like something to tell the trainers or teachers what their learners should become able to accomplish. This sort of statement of learning outcomes is quite unfriendly and remote if read by learners themselves, so I'll recommend sticking to the more personal and involving kind of learning outcomes, such as my earlier examples.

Objectives terminology

Elsewhere (please see Bibliography) you can find detailed descriptions of the terminology (or jargon) associated with behavioural objectives. For the present, the following is all that you may wish to see. Based on the work of Bloom and Mager, objectives are often classified into three overlapping 'domains' as follows:

- cognitive (knowledge, thinking, and so on)
- affective (feelings, attitudes, and so on)
- psychomotor (practical skills, and so on)

The domains themselves can be subdivided into 'hierarchies', for example:

Cognitive
knowledge
comprehension
application
analysis
synthesis
evaluation

Affective
receiving
responding
valuing
organizing
characterizing

The key word in any objective is the verb which describes exactly what sort of action the intended learning outcome is to be. 'Taxonomies' of objectives-verbs are available in print. There are problems however – one being that the various categories overlap so much. Another is that words like 'analysis' and 'synthesis' mean different things to different people. If an objective is to serve a useful purpose, its meaning should be clear to all and beyond dispute.

In this chapter, I'm putting the jargon on one side and concentrating on some down-to-earth criteria for making objectives and other learning-outcomes descriptors as useful as possible to *learners*. (They don't need or want to know which domain or hierarchy an objective lies in.) If you glance back at the objectives I started this chapter with, I hope you'll see that they are more specific than the aim. It's easier to tell from the objectives exactly what's involved. In fact, the term 'specific objectives' is quite commonly used. I hope you'll also find the objectives of this chapter meaningful and relevant to your purposes in using this book.

How specific?

One way of thinking about aims and objectives is as statements of intent with different 'sharpness'. In other words, an aim is not at all sharp, and an objective is much more so. We've seen that an objective is some kind of statement of the 'learning outcome' that is intended. This is sometimes referred to as the 'performance'. It's possible to make learning outcomes even clearer by referring to the 'conditions' under which the performance is to be achieved. So phrases such as the following may be slipped into learning outcomes when necessary:

> under exam conditions
> using your textbooks
> under laboratory conditions
> working as part of a team
> using a digital voltmeter

A final dimension can be added. The 'standard' of performance may sometimes need to be spelled out. So phrases such as these could be used:

> to four decimal places
> at least eight correct out of ten
> in 30 minutes or less
> in around 500 words

However, if all the conditions and standards were spelled out in every single objective, it would get longwinded and boring for learners. I suggest including information about conditions and standards only when the learners need to know such information. The main thing is for your learners to know exactly what you mean each time they see an objective.

Competence descriptors

'Competence statements' are increasingly used to define the learning outcomes that learners are meant to develop their ability to demonstrate. Competence statements are generally 'can do' statements. For example, a competent writer of open learning materials may be expected to be heading towards the following competences:

- can design learning packages which are attractive, helping learners to want to learn from them
- can design learning materials based on learners having the opportunity to learn by doing
- can write responses to self-assessment questions and other exercises so that learners have plenty of opportunity to receive feedback on their progress
- can incorporate into learning packages opportunities for learners to digest what they have mastered.

The above list would be a very broad indication of some of the skills or competences that a successful open learning writer would demonstrate. Of course, the use of the word 'can' is not necessary – after all, it's more important to describe what competent writers actually *do*, rather than merely what they might be able to do. Therefore, the list could be edited to provide broad statements of the relevant competences as follows:

■ designs learning packages which are attractive, helping learners to want to learn from them
■ designs learning materials based on learners having the opportunity to learn by doing
■ writes responses to self-assessment questions and other exercises, so that learners have plenty of opportunity to receive feedback on their progress
■ incorporates into learning packages opportunities for learners to digest what they have mastered.

As mentioned already, however relevant the above competence expressions are, they are still broad. They're still more like aims than objectives. To spell out the detail, 'performance criteria' or 'performance indicators' are needed. The following is an attempt to attach just three performance indicators to each of the above broad competence statements (an exhaustive description would require several more performance indicators under each statement of competence).

■ can design learning packages which are attractive, helping learners to want to learn from them
  – writes interesting introductions, which whet learners' appetites to go further
  – uses a pleasant tone and style of writing, so that learners feel comfortable with the materials
  – expresses learning outcomes clearly and without jargon, so that learners know exactly where they're heading.
■ can design learning materials based on learners having the opportunity to learn by doing
  – uses self-assessment questions widely, so that learners have ample opportunity to practise relevant skills
  – designs tutor-marked assignments so learners can practise in a more formal way, and gain credit for the skills and knowledge they acquire
  – avoids 'telling' learners things, when it is possible for learners to find out for themselves by solving problems, or 'having a go', helping learners to develop a feeling of ownership of their developing skills or knowledge.
■ can write responses to self-assessment questions and other exercises so that learners have plenty of opportunity to receive feedback on their progress
  – designs structured feedback to learners on what they have just done rather than simply providing answers to the self-assessment questions

- gives learners the opportunity to find out the answer to the questions 'Was I right?' and 'If not, why not?'
- designs tutor-marked assignments, not simply to test learners, but as an opportunity for them to benefit from the sort of feedback which needs human judgement and skills.

■ can incorporate into learning packages opportunities for learners to digest what they have mastered
  - uses summaries and reviews to give learners the chance to consolidate what they have already mastered
  - incorporates 'check your learning' quizzes and exercises, to help learners discover exactly what they may need to consolidate further
  - includes activities and exercises which give learners further practice in using the skills and knowledge they have gained.

You can see from the way that the above list is growing that competence descriptors are in effect doing the same job as lists of 'sharp' objectives. The performance criteria are giving the parameters, helping learners (in our case, writers) gain a better picture of what it will be like to have successfully developed and demonstrated the specified competences.

Range statements

These can be added to the developing description of intended learning outcomes to specify some of the more quantitative aspects of the intended outcomes. Range statements can also be designed to give further information about the level or quality of the performance which is to be given. When performance is to be graded (for example, in terms of 'pass', 'merit' and 'distinction' as used in many vocational qualifications) it is appropriate for the range statements to give learners an accurate picture of the respective levels of performance they may need to demonstrate having achieved the respective grades. Our example of the competences that are relevant to open learning writing do not extend readily to grading, but the following attempt to add this sort of detail may give you an inkling of the way range statements may work.

■ can write responses to self-assessment questions and other exercises so that learners have plenty of opportunity to receive feedback on their progress
  - designs structured feedback to learners on what they have just done rather than simply providing answers to the self-assessment questions
  - gives learners the opportunity to find out the answer to the questions 'Was I right?' and 'If not, why not?'
  - designs tutor-marked assignments, not simply to test learners, but as an opportunity for them to benefit from the sort of feedback which needs human judgement and skills.

Range statements showing grading criteria

'Pass'   Designs a selection of self-assessment questions and responses, giving learners useful feedback on their progress, and adds a tutor-marked assignment.

'Merit'   Designs a selection of self-assessment questions and responses, using at least three different structured-question formats, which give learners useful feedback on their progress. Designs a tutor-marked assignment and model answer to assist tutor marking.

'Distinction'   Designs a selection of self-assessment questions, using at least six different structured-question formats, and designs responses which give learners useful feedback on their progress, especially when they got a question 'wrong'. Designs a tutor-marked assignment and marking scheme to assist tutor marking, and a model answer in the form of 'answer plus commentary' which could be used by tutors to respond to learners' anticipated difficulties on the assignment.

As you will see from this final version of the 'feedback' competence descriptor, there is now a great deal of information there about the nature, quality and quantity of the intended learning outcomes. In particular, the range statement information gives a lot of additional detail about the nature of the evidence which will, in due course, be assessed. However, may I stress that awarding 'pass', 'merit' or 'distinction' to open learning writers would be considerably more complex than my attempt above may suggest; I simply wished the example to demonstrate how the additional information in range statements can help learners find out yet more about what is to be expected of them.

By now you will appreciate that aims, behavioural objectives, competence statements, performance criteria, range statements and so on are all serving the same purpose of clarifying 'where learners are heading'. Rather than repeatedly name all of these kinds of 'intended learning outcome', for the remainder of this chapter I will simply use the terms 'learning outcomes' or 'objectives', leaving it to you to extend the thinking behind the discussion to each and every way of showing learners where they're heading.

Whose learning outcomes should they be?

The learner's, of course! Objectives should be used so as to be as meaningful and helpful as possible to each learner. I make the point because so often we see sets of objectives that seem designed to help anyone but the learner! Let's look briefly at the objectives of some of the other people involved.

Syllabus designers' objectives

Some objectives seem to be simply ways in which syllabus designers have broken down the content of each topic. Fine, if such objectives manage to help the learner too. But the danger is that such objectives are usually written in language that the learner hasn't yet learned about – and this can be very intimidating.

Teachers' objectives

Breaking syllabus matter down into learning outcomes can certainly help teachers structure their courses. But it's surprising how often the teachers don't let the learners in on the learning outcomes! It's almost as if some teachers wish to keep the 'expected learning outcomes' secret from their learners. Why?

Assessment objectives

A list of learning outcomes can certainly be a useful frame of reference for structuring exams and tests. After all, the learning outcomes should be spelling out exactly what the learners should be able to do. But again, the purpose of writing a set of learning outcomes is not solely to make it easier to write tests and exams. It's much better if the *learners* can use the learning outcomes too, to help them to prepare successfully for exams and tests. Open learners may be doing much of the studying on their own. In conventional classes, a teacher often gives what amounts to learning outcomes in informal asides ('What I really want you to become able to do is . . .'). This sort of elaboration of learning outcomes is of course very useful. The isolated open learner needs this kind of help all the more. Let's explore in more detail some reasons for going to the trouble of writing learning outcomes specially for open learners.

Why design learning outcomes or competence descriptors for open learners?

Listed below are half a dozen reasons for going to the trouble of making learning outcomes directly useful to open learners.

To show learners exactly what they're to do

- Alert them to challenges. If you write, for example, 'this one's a tricky one', learners will pull out all the stops to try and master it. If they're not alerted to the challenge, they may come to a dead stop when they find it's tricky.
- Alert them to standards to be reached. Open learners may not be able to ask 'What exactly have I to do to pass?'; the learning outcomes can make this quite clear to them.
- Alert them to *why* they're doing so-and-so. In 'live' classes, someone will ask 'Why do we need this?' The open learner needs to know this too; learning outcomes can help to explain why various tasks are set and so on.

To show learners what they've achieved

■ Give them a frame of reference to measure their progress. Open learners don't want to have to wait till they're formally tested to find out what they can and can't do. A good set of learning outcomes gives them the means to check for themselves how they're getting on.

To show learners what they've yet to master

■ When not yet successful, show them where the outstanding issues, problems or needs are. If they know exactly what the problem is, they're more than halfway towards solving it. The biggest danger is when learners have problems they *don't* know about. Objectives can help them see exactly what their problem areas are.

To build their self-confidence

■ Allow them to see what they have already mastered. The feeling of having achieved the first few learning outcomes successfully can be a big morale boost to open learners working on their own.

■ Let them see that progress is achieved a step at a time, even when the subject matter is demanding. A primary task may look formidable, but when it is split into a number of simpler steps, it becomes much more manageable. If learning outcomes allow the open learners to see the smaller steps in advance, they're less likely to baulk as a difficult task comes along.

To let them see why they're being asked to do things (such as self-assessment questions, activities, assignments and so on)

■ Objectives help show them the purposes of building-in all the interactive elements common in good open learning materials.

To allow the 'end-product' of the package to be measured

■ Let the learners see just where they will be when they have completed the package. If they know where they're heading, they'll feel more at home all the way through their learning.
■ Let other people (for example employers) see whether the package measures up to the training needs of employees. People deciding whether or not to select a particular package look hard at the learning outcomes.

All the above reasons for writing learning outcomes are connected with the learners. However, there are other good reasons for using learning outcomes, not least that they can help in the whole process of designing open learning materials (see Chapter 2). In particular, a well-formulated set of learning outcomes is the basis for structuring learning activities and self-assessment questions and responses. The clearer the intended learning outcomes are, the easier it is to fight the tendency to run off at tangents when writing the text.

How can learning outcomes help writers?

Suppose you've already mapped out a series of learning objectives, before starting to put together a piece of open learning material. Here are some ways that the learning outcomes may make your task easier, and your writing more rapid and efficient.

- You'll be less likely to go off on tangents while writing text. The learning outcomes are a useful reminder of what your learners need to achieve. Anything not directly connected with an objective is probably not needed by them, however much you're itching to write it.
- The set of learning outcomes provides the best possible framework for your design of self-assessment questions and activities. It's useful to try to cover each of the learning outcomes with such learner activities.
- If you're also going to design assignment questions (for example, for tutor-marked assignments), the learning outcomes help you to keep firmly on target. They allow you to design assignments which test the whole of the content rather than isolated parts of it.
- The hardest part of writing open learning material is simply getting started. If you've got a set of learning outcomes, you don't have to start at the beginning. You can pick any of the learning outcomes, and write a piece of text leading the learner towards achieving it, and SAQs and responses to give the learner practice at achieving it.

In Chapter 2, we've already seen how well-defined learning outcomes can lie at the heart of an efficient strategy for designing open learning materials, and in the next chapter we'll explore in detail how to move from known learning outcomes to learning-by-doing activities for learners, and feedback responses so they can find out how their learning is proceeding.

Mapping out learning outcomes

What to include, and what not to include, is the issue. It's a case of deciding what the learner *needs to know*. If there's an exam standard to be reached, that provides most of the detail about exactly what learners should be able to do at the end of their study. There may well be many things that could be classified as 'nice to know'. It may be worth including some of these things as learning outcomes. However, if the learners are to make best use of your learning outcomes, it's best that the learning outcomes tell them very clearly the things they *need* to become able to do.

Making learning outcomes useful to open learners

At last, you may be thinking, we're back to the title of this chapter! But by now, I hope you can see how we're aiming to make learning outcomes useful to learners rather than merely useful to syllabus designers, teachers, examiners or open learning module writers. If learning outcomes aren't useful, what happens is that they're simply skimmed over – or ignored – by open learners. This does indeed happen with many existing learning materials. So, to make sure that your learning outcomes are used, we need to make sure that they're intelligible, and serving purposes that your learners will find useful. Here are some general suggestions.

Don't just list the learning outcomes

Cross-reference them to self-assessment questions, text, assignment questions and so on. Let the learners know where they fit in. Printed asides such as 'This question gives you the chance to check how you're getting on regarding Objective 3 of this section' or 'This Activity will help you collect evidence so you can demonstrate your achievement of Competence Statement 4.2, especially concerning the first two performance criteria' can be useful pointers to learners.

Don't list too many learning outcomes at a time

It's said that we only notice half a dozen things from a list, however long. It's best to introduce the learning outcomes a few at a time. (Of course the whole lot can be listed as an appendix at the back of the module, or published separately in a little booklet which can serve as a 'route map' to the learning programme.)

Make learning outcomes personal

Write 'You'll be able to...' not 'The expected learning outcome is that the learner will...'. Learners working on their own prefer the informal approach. They need to feel involved. 'You'll be able to...' may even be preferable to 'You will be able to...'. Splitting hairs? To me, the latter can sometimes imply 'we have ways of making you able to...'.

Avoid unnecessary jargon

If possible, avoid terms that your learners don't already know. A forbidding phrase or term may stop learners from pressing on. Put things simply in the pre-section learning outcomes, you can always list them rigorously at the end of the section, once the learner knows the jargon.

Relate learning outcomes to the experience of learners

Don't keep learning outcomes abstract. You can often add in brackets something like ('for example, you can . . .') which helps your learners see exactly where the objective fits into their view of the subject.

Make them specific enough

Your learners need to be able to tell when they've achieved each objective. So rather than say 'List features of so-and-so', it could be more useful to say 'List half a dozen features of so-and-so'.

Avoid vague words like 'know', and 'understand'

Spell out the things the learners will be able to *do* when they 'understand' so-and-so. Whenever someone in one of my writing workshops uses 'understand' in an objective, I reply 'but how would you *tell* whether they understood it?' They always reply 'Well, by *doing* this and that, or explaining so-and-so . . .'. My reply then is to encourage them to put these words into the objective rather than 'understand'. (You can get away with such words as 'know' and 'understand' in your list of aims, but they're not sharp enough for learning outcomes.)

Make them motivating and attractive

Try to make the learners *want* to achieve them. Try to 'sell' the learning outcomes to learners in terms of the benefits they will derive after achieving them. Even little additions such as 'This is a favourite exam question' can give learners extra incentive to master a particularly important objective.

Point out to learners the important ones

In a printed list of half a dozen learning outcomes, they may all *look* of equal stature. However, one of them may be crucial, others less so. A few words in brackets can tell learners about this. Otherwise, the danger with print or typescript remains that everything tends to look of equal importance.

Mention the tough ones

If a particular objective is likely to be a hard one to achieve, let the learners know this. With advance notice, they'll try all the harder when they come to it. They'll avoid the pain of suddenly hitting something difficult. When already alerted to a challenge, most learners pull out all the stops and try their hardest.

Return to the learning outcomes

For example, at the end of a piece of material, review the learning outcomes again. Remind your learners of the things they've been mastering. (Perhaps you'd like to take another look at the intended learning outcomes listed as objectives at the start of this chapter? How are you getting on with them?)

Make the learning outcomes match assessment requirements

This is probably the most important of all the criteria I've suggested. When the learners have mastered your learning outcomes as stated, they should automatically be able to do any exam question or assignment question correctly. Furthermore, they should *know* they can do so. If they can't, it's the fault of the learning outcomes writer, not the fault of the learners!

The suggestions I've made above may look rather demanding. However, the intention is that learning outcomes should be a useful tool – particularly for your learners themselves. Let's summarize the main points we've explored in the form of a checklist which you can apply to learning outcomes in open learning materials (whether designed by yourself or by others).

Checklist

Each statement of intended learning outcome should be:

- easily understood
- not too long
- unambiguous
- friendly and motivating
- not patronizing when simple
- not frightening when difficult
- clear and jargon-free
- linked to relevant sections of text
- related clearly to relevant learner activities
- clear in the description of the *evidence* that will prove it has been achieved
- expressed such that learners can themselves tell when they've achieved it.

The learning outcomes as a whole should be:

- not presented too many at a time
- not like the average objectives-based syllabus
- all-embracing (covering *everything* the learner is expected to master)
- relevant (not including things the learner isn't expected to master)
- cross-referenced to text and the rest of the material
- importance-graded (ie, the essential learning outcomes distinguishable by the learners from the more optional ones)
- usable as a checklist when the learners have completed their studies of the material concerned.

Conclusions

Objectives and other ways of expressing learning outcomes, when used well, are vital tools for showing your learners exactly what they're supposed to become able to do. In face-to-face teaching, students get all sorts of help regarding what they're supposed to be able to do. Learners ask questions, answer questions, listen to emphasis in tone of voice and so on. Open learners miss out on many of these sources of help, and therefore need all the guidance that a good set of learning outcomes can provide. An important additional dimension for open learning outcomes is the user-friendly one. That dimension is usually totally absent in the typical objectives-based syllabus. When designing learning outcomes for open learning, it's useful to imagine a typical learner asking you the following questions:

- What exactly will I be able to do when I've finished this module?
- Which bits do I really need to master to pass?
- What sorts of evidence will I need to produce to demonstrate I've achieved the learning outcomes?
- How will I know whether I'm heading for a good grade or not?
- Are there any difficult bits I should be watching out for?

Our objectives revisited

Now that you've worked through this chapter, ask yourself to what extent you feel you have achieved the objectives that we started out with.

Can you now:

- distinguish between aims and specific learning outcomes such as objectives?
- write clear, precise learning outcomes?
- explain the relationships between a competence statement, performance criteria and range statements?
- formulate learning outcomes which are directly helpful to learners – open learners in particular?
- use expressed learning outcomes to play a major role in open learning materials?

Chapter 4

Designing Self-assessment Questions and Feedback Responses

Abstract

In Chapters 1 and 2 we explored the importance of 'learning by doing' and 'receiving feedback' as key stages in the processes whereby people learn things successfully and develop positive feelings about their learning. In Chapter 3, we saw the usefulness of pinning down exactly what the intended learning outcomes are, and expressing these in ways that are useful to learners. The next logical steps are to translate the intended learning outcomes into 'learning by doing' opportunities, and to design structured feedback for learners so that they find out how their learning is going.

Objectives

When you've worked through this chapter, you should be able to:

- accept that self-assessment questions and responses (in one form or another) are at the heart of all high-quality open learning materials
- design self-assessment questions which are clear, attractive and, above all, useful learning experiences for your open learners
- compose responses which perform a useful teaching function.

'How am I doing?'

Perhaps the greatest need of open learners working on their own is that of knowing how they are getting on. Self-assessment questions are at the heart of any good open learning package. In particular, the responses learners receive when they've had a go at such questions have two vital roles to play: addressing the questions 'Was I right?' and 'If not, why not?' I should explain at once that there are several other names for what we're calling self-assessment questions: For instance:

- exercise
- activity
- DIY (do-it-yourself)
- ITQ (in-text questions)
- 'check your progress' activities
- self-test.

All these things are designed to achieve the same things on behalf of open learners as self-assessment questions and responses. In conventional courses, learners have regular feedback from tutors – and above all they can compare their progress with each other's. Open learners wish to find out how well (or otherwise) their studies are going before subjecting themselves to more formal judgements based on written assignments and tutor feedback – or before going in for exams. That's where self-assessment questions come in.

In Chapter 2 we explored strategies for putting together open learning materials, starting with the intended learning outcomes and deriving from these things for learners to do so that they could learn by doing and gain feedback. We noted that sometimes learners would need human skills, experience and judgement to reply individually to the way they had addressed tasks, and that such tasks would be suitable for tutor-marked assignments rather than self-assessment questions. In this chapter, we will concentrate on things where structured feedback can be given (in print, or on the screen in computer-based learning). This structured feedback does, of course, still require human skills, experience and judgment, but in the design of the questions and responses, rather than as one-off responses to individual pieces of work done by learners.

What is a self-assessment question?

A self-assessment question asks learners to *do* something. It may well ask learners to recall something they already learned from the materials or textbooks. But there are many sorts of self-assessment questions, going far beyond mere recall, and serving many purposes. Here are some of the kinds of activity self-assessment questions require of learners:

- *making decisions:* for example, picking the correct option in multiple-choice questions
- *application:* using things they have learned to solve problems
- *extending:* using what they already know, plus their thinking skills, to go a bit further than the materials have already taken them
- *drawing or sketching:* for example, adding labels to diagrams
- *diagnosis:* for example, working out what is wrong or what is missing in some given information, textual or visual

■ *guessing:* for example, having a go at working out why something happens.

These are just some of the things self-assessment questions can do. But there's more to it than just *doing* something. When learners have finished having a go at a self-assessment question, they then turn to the response composed by the author. (In computer-based open learning systems, the response will usually appear on the monitor screen after learners have keyed in a choice of option, or an answer.) This is where the self-assessment comes in. Now they find out how right (or how wrong) their own efforts have been.

What do learners want to know?

Quite simply, learners who have attempted self-assessment questions want to know the following:

■ 'Was I right?'
■ 'If not, why not? What went wrong? What should I do about it?'

What is the role of the response?

Suppose, for example, a learner has picked an option in a multiple-choice question. The learner is either right or wrong. The learner then turns to the back of the module where the responses to self-assessment questions are collected together. The response needs to be of value to learners who picked the right option or one of the wrong options. To achieve this the response needs to do several things.

Responding to learners who choose the right option

Most learners appreciate a message of congratulation of some sort, such as:

■ Well done
■ Excellent
■ Good
■ That's correct
■ Splendid
■ You're quite right
■ Spot on!
■ Congratulations!
■ Great!
■ Right, of course!

The response then needs to continue by reminding learners exactly *what* they got right – reinforcement.

Responding to learners who choose an incorrect option

Here, the response needs to give some sort of message of sympathy. Learners need to feel that any mistake they made was reasonable. They also need to find out two further things from the response:

- *why* they may have made the mistake
- what the correct answer should have been.

There are plenty of messages of sympathy to choose from. Here are some examples:

- This was a tricky question
- Most people find this hard at first
- I used to get this wrong myself at first
- Don't worry, you'll soon get used to this sort of question
- I'm glad you picked this option, because I can now explain to you exactly what to beware of in questions of this sort.

Since multiple-choice questions are very versatile as self-assessment questions, we'll look at them in detail later in this chapter.

If you're now beginning to think that the responses are actually more important than the questions themselves, well done – so do I! The responses reflect the things you would have said to your learners if you were looking over their shoulders as they got things right, or made their mistakes.

The comfort of privacy

One of the greatest advantages of open learning materials is that learners can make their mistakes in private. No one else need know they ever made mistakes. Learning from mistakes means that when the time comes for 'public performance' such as tutor-marked assignments, test or exams, the same old mistakes are much less likely. If there are lots of self-assessment questions, learners can go back and retry them time and time again over the weeks until they build up both speed and confidence at handling them correctly.

In the last chapter, we saw how valuable expressions of intended learning outcomes can be to open learners. It's very important that self-assessment questions are linked closely to these intended outcomes. After all, the self-assessment questions are asking learners to practise doing the various things involved in achieving the outcomes. Therefore, learners who have achieved all of the learning outcomes should expect to be able to tackle all the self-assessment questions correctly. More importantly, learners who master all the self-assessment questions should automatically be able to demonstrate their achievement of all the learning outcomes. This also means that learners who handle all your self-assessment questions well should also be able to do well in any assignments or exams. If they don't, your self-assessment questions and responses are missing either crucial learning-by-doing practice, or important elements of feedback needed by learners.

Privacy and 'cheating'?

When printed responses to self-assessment questions are included in open learning packages, there's no way that we can prevent learners from 'cheating' by looking at the responses before they've attempted the questions. However perhaps this should not be regarded as cheating in any case – it is one way of learning. That said, it's possible to reduce the chances that learners will look at responses prematurely. The most important way of doing this is to make sure that the responses are not too convenient to find. For example, it's little use at all if the responses are in sight while learners are doing the questions, yet a surprising number of open learning packages contain questions and activities which the learners can see the answers to if their eyes stray a little further down the page! It's also too 'convenient' if the response to a self-assessment question is just over the page – the temptation is too great.

Probably the safest policy is to cluster the responses at the end of the package or at the end of particular sections in the package. Then, 'cheating' has to be done quite deliberately and is therefore less likely.

What purposes should SAQs and responses serve

We've already established that the prime role of self-assessment questions and responses is to give learners the chance to learn by doing, and to give them rapid feedback on what they do. Before we start to explore various types of self-assessment question, I'd like you to think a bit more about the purposes that the questions – and particularly their responses – should serve. I list below some key purposes of self-assessment questions and responses.

To give learners opportunities to learn by doing

Merely reading can so easily be passive. Self-assessment questions involve thinking, making decisions, practising, calculating and all sorts of other active processes.

To confirm to your learners what they have already mastered

This helps them to build their confidence, and also helps them to see what important in their learning. We've already emphasized the vital role receiving feedback plays in the way that people learn.

To help learners discover what they have not yet mastered

Once learners know what the dangers are, they're in a much better position to get to grips with them. The real danger is 'not knowing what you don't yet know

To 'catch' things before they slip

It's all too easy to understand something one minute, and for it to be gone the next. Self-assessment questions give learners the chance to consolidate their learning before it evaporates. That extra few minutes spent reflecting on what has been learned is one of the most important stages in the learning process – I introduced the term 'digesting' for it in Chapter 1.

To help learners see what's important

If there are several self-assessment questions about a particular topic, learners quickly latch on to the fact that they really need to try to master that topic.

To 'translate' the intended learning outcomes

Self-assessment questions spell out to learners exactly what sorts of things they need to be able to do to demonstrate their achievement of the expressed learning outcomes. We noted in Chapter 3 how complicated and longwinded it can become to express these outcomes completely unambiguously and fully (especially in competence terms, with all the performance criteria and range statements). Self-assessment questions can in their own way show learners exactly what each learning outcome really means.

To develop learners' confidence

Many learners, especially those working on their own, need to have their self-confidence increased. When learners tackle most of the self-assessment questions correctly, they become much more confident. There is no harm slipping in a self-assessment question now and then which *everyone* should get right.

To give learners practice at responding to questions

Many kinds of formal assessment depend on being able to answer questions – often in writing. Self-assessment questions give learners such practice in the comfort of privacy where no one else sees their mistakes.

To prevent learners getting bored or 'passive'

Working on one's own, if boredom sets in, it's all too easy for attention to wander. Self-assessment questions bring back learners' attention.

To show learners 'where they're at'

Open learners want to know how well or how badly they're doing. Self-assessment questions give them the chance to measure their progress – again, in private.

To help learners choose the right pace

If learners are forging ahead quickly, *and* getting all the self-assessment questions right, they can be confident that the fast pace is all right. If quite a few self-assessment questions cause errors, learners can tell that the pace needs to be reduced, and some revision is needed.

Quite a list, isn't it? This is because open learning (at its best) is highly learner centred, and there's no better way of getting your learners involved than by asking them to do all sorts of things and by using the responses to provide them with detailed feedback on what they do.

How best can SAQs and responses serve their purposes?

Let's now move on to look at some general principles which can ensure that self assessment questions achieve their purposes.

Start using them as soon as you can

There's no need to wait until page 10 to pose the first self-assessment question. You can pose a self-assessment question even before you've told your learner anything! For example:

See if you can guess which of the following is the reason why so-and-so does such-and-such.

This sort of question wouldn't threaten learners who don't know: you said 'guess'. Then, they find out from the responses anything they didn't know.

Use them often

A useful rule is to have a self-assessment question in view on each double-page spread. A double-page spread of pure text is very good at causing learners to shut the book!

Don't just use SAQs for 'recall'

You can get learners to predict, select, guess, calculate, apply, diagnose, draw, add labels, fill in blanks and so on. There are plenty of things that don't involve looking back and merely re-reading what the correct answer is!

Build in plenty of variety

Use different types of self-assessment question every now and then: it gives your learners a change. (We'll explore several types briefly in this chapter.)

Use SAQs to address 'real learner errors'

There's not much point throwing in incorrect options which wouldn't be chosen by anyone.

Compose responses, not just answers

I've already stressed the importance of this in general terms in Chapter 2; we'll explore this in more detail later in the present chapter.

Types of SAQ

There are many types of self-assessment question. However, we can explore many of the uses of such questions and responses by thinking about some of the following eight main types:

- multiple choice
- matching
- filling in blanks
- sequencing
- true–false
- completion
- fault-finding
- open-ended.

I'll go into some detail with the first of these types – multiple-choice questions. For the remainder, I'll merely give a few guidelines, as the principles for multiple-choice questions can easily be extended to most of the other types. Finally, I'll prescribe a rather demanding list of criteria which you can use to measure the quality of the self-assessment questions and responses in open learning materials.

Despite what I said about putting the responses to self-assessment questions out of sight so that learners have the chance to attempt them properly before being alerted to the correct answers, in my examples in this chapter I'm putting the responses immediately after the questions so that you can see more easily how I'm trying to relate the two components.

Black and white, or shades of grey?

In the examples I've chosen for this chapter, I've tended to stick to 'black-and-white' questions; in other words, questions where a particular answer is 'right' and all other answers are 'wrong' in some way. That said, each of the formats can easily be extended to situations where there are 'shades of grey'. For example, in multiple-choice questions, there can be a 'best' option, a 'next-best' option, an 'adequate' option, a 'not-so-good' option, and a 'poor' option. The responses to

the questions can give information about *why* each option falls into th
appropriate orders of preference.

Multiple-choice questions

These consist of a stem (the bit at the beginning) and some options (usually fou
or five – but it doesn't really matter how many). One of the options, called th
key, is either absolutely correct, or the best of the options. The incorrect option
in multiple choice questions are sometimes called 'distractors', but, as we'll see
this isn't really appropriate for self-assessment question purposes. The incorrec
options are not there simply to distract learners – they're there to 'catch' learner
who've made anticipated mistakes, so that useful teaching messages can be buil
into the responses to these options. With any multiple choice question (self
assessment or exam) it's important that learners don't have unintentional clue
as to the right and wrong options. It's surprisingly easy to give such clue
accidentally. If you write such a question, you'll probably be the last person t
spot any clues!

Tips for writing multiple-choice SAQs

Here are some suggestions to help your questions and responses be as valuabl
as possible to your learners:

■ Keep the stem as clear and unambiguous as possible; this usually means kee
it as short as practicable.
■ Make sure that learners know whether to pick *one* correct option, or the *be*
option, or *more than one* correct option, and so on
■ It's best to avoid the following sorts of stem:
Which of the following is *not* an example of . . . ?
Which of the following is an *incorrect* form of . . . ?
Which of the following is the *exception* to the rule of . . . ?
Even when capitals or italics are used to emphasize the 'negative' aspect c
such questions, learners still tend to look for the thing that is 'right' c
'correct', rather than exceptions, errors and so on.
■ It may be a good idea from time to time to get your learners thinking abou
the incorrect options; for example:
'In each of the following questions, select the correct (or best) option, an
also try to decide what is wrong with the other options. Then check th
responses to *all* the options, and find out how right you are.'
■ Make the incorrect options as plausible as you can: if there's an 'obvious!
wrong' option, it won't be serving any useful purpose – unless from time t
time you are able to use a 'funny' option to bring a smile to the faces of you
learners.
■ Try to choose incorrect options which represent *likely learner errors*. In you
responses you can then address each such likely error separately and directl

In other words, choose incorrect options where you can make the response have a useful teaching function.

- Don't write the stem so that it ends with the indefinite article 'a' or 'an'. This obviously gives learners a clue, directing them to an answer which begins with, respectively, a consonant or a vowel.

  Example of what to avoid!

  'The word "effective" is an:

  A   noun

  B   verb

  C   adjective

  D   conjunction.'

- Make the options of roughly equal length. If one is much longer than the rest, learners will probably think it must be the correct one.

- Avoid using any 'leading' words from the stem in the key. For example, if the stem asks 'Which is the most useful form of . . . ?' take care that 'useful' (or a similar word) doesn't stray into any of the options, particularly the *key* (the correct option).

- Avoid one option being more 'qualified' by conditions than the others. An option that looks 'tighter' will usually seem more likely to be correct, although learners may not understand why.

- Be careful with the following sorts of words:

usually	never
often	always
sometimes	all
seldom	none

  Words from the left-hand list shouldn't be mixed with those from the right-hand list in a series of options. Any word from the left-hand list will seem much more probable than words from the right-hand list. This is because we can rarely be as definite as to say 'never', 'always' and so on – there's *always* an exception or two! Of course, you can use all the words in the left-hand list to make up a set of options – or indeed all the words from the right-hand list.

- If you're using a series of multiple-choice questions, make sure that options (a), (b), (c) and so on come up with roughly equal frequency as *keys*. If it has been a very long time since there was a (d), learners who are unsure will tend to go for (d)!

- With a series of multiple-choice questions, make sure that there isn't a pattern. Suppose you met eight questions, and sorted out (correctly) the first seven as follows, what would you guess for question 8 if you didn't know the right answer?

  1   (a)

  2   (b)

  3   (c)

  4   (d)

  5   (a)

6 (b)
7 (c)
8 ?

Most people would guess (d). Again, this seems an obvious point, but in practice (especially in multiple-choice exams) it has caused problems.

So, you can see that it's a good deal more demanding to design a good multiple choice self-assessment question than a simple exam question. The crucial part of any self-assessment question is the response, and you can't respond to mere throwaway incorrect options. Now let's explore in a bit more detail the business of composing useful responses to multiple-choice questions (remembering that the principles of providing feedback responses will be relevant to responses to other kinds of self-assessment questions too).

Responses to multiple-choice SAQs

Remember that learners can't be forced into doing all your self-assessment questions. It's possible for learners to skip them – a consequence of working in the comfort of privacy. The best way to ensure that learners do all of your questions is to make the responses so useful and interesting that they feel deprived if they skip them. The following suggestions are all ways of helping learners to get the most out of your responses.

- Learners want to know straight away whether the chosen option was right or not. You can do one or both of two things to help:
  - start the response to the whole question with something like 'The correct answer is (c)', then go on to discuss each option in turn
  - make it quite clear at the very start of each response whether the option was correct or not; for example:
    A Not quite right: you may have thought that . . .
    B That's correct: it's true that . . .
- Make sure that your responses to correct options don't get boring. As I said earlier, there are hundreds of 'messages of congratulation' to choose from so don't say 'Well done' every time.
- If learners pick an incorrect option, your response should help them to:
  - not to feel complete idiots
  - find out what the correct answer should have been
  - find out what went wrong, leading them to pick an incorrect option.
  I mentioned earlier various ways of softening the blow for the learner who has just made a mistake, by using phrases like 'Don't worry, you'll soon get used to this'.
- Give some sort of reward to learners who pick the correct option. I don't just mean give some praise; I mean give a little extra information of some sort. For example: 'Very good. This also means that . . .'. This helps to ensure that learners feel it is worth checking the responses, even when they are sure

they've picked the right option. (If they stop checking, they might not discover their mistakes, thinking they are right when they are not.)

■ Make sure that learners are reminded of *what* was right or wrong. Learners may not be reading the question itself when they are looking at your response. They may have forgotten what the question was! So, remind them in the response. For example:

'Sorry, but density is in fact mass divided by volume. To have picked this option you must have thought it was volume divided by mass – don't worry, you'll be having plenty of practice at this later in the module.'

Good responses to multiple choice questions are therefore very much more than:

'(B)   No, (A) was correct'.

Yet so often, this is all one finds. I've discussed multiple-choice questions and responses at some length. However, as I said, much of the advice given here applies equally to other types of self-assessment question. Before leaving multiple-choice entirely, I'd like to summarize the particular advantages that such questions can have as a self-assessment device.

Some advantages of multiple-choice SAQs

Multiple choice questions are often regarded with suspicion in educational circles. They are thought to be unreliable in exams. But the reason for that is usually that the questions have not been adequately piloted before exam use. Reliable questions can indeed be designed. While the use of multiple-choice questions in exams may have its limitations, in *self-assessment* they are very useful. Let's explore some of their advantages in open learning materials.

- You can respond individually, and directly, to different learners making different errors.
- You can brief learners not just to pick out the correct option each time, but to find out what is wrong with each of the incorrect options. This can help learners take note of mistakes to steer clear of.
- It's much easier to write responses to multiple-choice questions than to open-ended questions. For example, if you asked the open-ended question 'What are the three main causes of corrosion?', you wouldn't know what learners might write in answer to this. All you could do is give an answer, not really a *response*.

However, if you asked 'Which of the following options lists the three main causes of corrosion?', you could then respond about why each of the incorrect options *didn't* list the main causes of corrosion.

While multiple choice can easily be used in self-assessment questions for options which are either right (key) or wrong (incorrect options), they are also very useful for 'shades of grey'. One can ask 'Which of the following do you think is the *best* reason for . . . ?' The responses to each option can then discuss any good points wrapped up in the incorrect options, as well as pointing out the arguments for the key being the best choice.

Example

SELF-ASSESSMENT QUESTION I

Which of the following are good reasons for using multiple choice questions in open learning materials?

A   They're easy to write.
B   It's easy to write responses to them.
C   You can give direct feedback to each learner.
D   They 'force' learners to make decisions.

RESPONSE TO SELF-ASSESSMENT QUESTION I

The best reasons are C and D.

A   *They're easy to write.* Not really! It takes quite a long time to work out a series of useful options – throwaway options don't serve any real purpose.
B   *It's easy to write responses to them.* No, the hardest part of designing multiple-choice self-assessment questions is writing the responses. It's no use just telling learners what the best or 'correct' option is, they need to know what's wrong with all the other options.
C   *You can give direct feedback to each learner.* Yes indeed, this is one of the strongest advantages of multiple-choice questions. Each response can be designed primarily for the learners who made the particular choices included in the question, and you can therefore reply separately to various mistakes or assumptions.
D   *They 'force' learners to make decisions.* This too is an advantage of multiple-choice questions. Until learners have committed themselves on one way or another, they're not ready to benefit from the feedback you provide in your response.

Matching

Unlike multiple-choice questions, 'matching' questions do not have the advantage that it is possible to respond to everything that learners may do with the question. However, it is possible to provide an 'answer', which is turned into something more like a 'response' by adding comments pertaining to the most likely causes of error or confusion. The example below is a very primitive form of a matching question.

SELF-ASSESSMENT QUESTION 2

In the following lists, connect each county to the town where the corresponding local government offices are located.

Dorset	Cardiff
Suffolk	Taunton
Somerset	Aberdeen
Grampian	Dorchester
Mid Glamorgan	Ipswich

It is best that when learners see the response to any sort of self-assessment question they are reminded exactly what the question asked them to do. It is important that what they see resembles what they did. For example, in the matching question above, the most likely thing that learners may do is draw lines connecting the various towns and counties. The best way for them to check whether they were correct in their connections is to show them a response of exactly the same format, this time with the lines drawn in for them. (The response would, of course, be separated from the question itself – for example, at the end of the section, chapter, or module.)

RESPONSE TO SELF-ASSESSMENT QUESTION 2

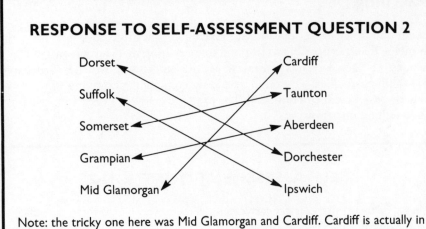

Note: the tricky one here was Mid Glamorgan and Cardiff. Cardiff is actually in South Glamorgan, but Mid Glamorgan's County Hall is still in Cardiff, as a consequence of local government reorganization splitting the old county of Glamorgan into three parts (the other is West Glamorgan, main town Swansea).

However, once the learner has paired off the first four pairs, the last one is left over, 'redundant', and is therefore obvious. A way round this is to use some added distractors. The question could then become:

SELF-ASSESSMENT QUESTION 3

In the following lists, connect as many as possible of the counties to the towns or cities where the corresponding local government offices are located. Which are the 'unrelated' places in each list?

Dorset	Cardiff
Suffolk	Taunton
Tyne and Wear	Gateshead
Somerset	Aberdeen
East Sussex	Sunderland
Grampian	Dorchester
Mid Glamorgan	Ipswich

The response could then be along the lines of the following:

RESPONSE TO SELF-ASSESSMENT QUESTION 3

In the following lists, connect as many as possible of the counties to the towns or cities where the corresponding local government offices are located. Which are the 'unrelated' places in each list?

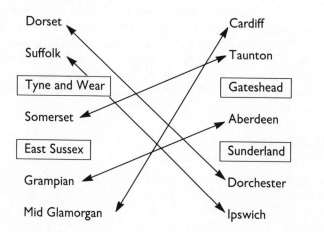

Note that Tyne and Wear corresponds with Newcastle upon Tyne, which also serves as the local government centre for Sunderland and Gateshead. East Sussex corresponds to Brighton.

Matching questions can be quite useful even when the final pair to be matched obvious; for example, when the fine differences between a set of similar things re to be learned. Matching each of the things to its exact definition is a useful ay of drawing attention to the fact that similarities exist, and the differences eed to be learned. A criticism often levelled against matching questions (and any other structured or closed forms) is that the information is all there in the uestion; the learners don't have to recall things.

In the defence of structured questions, I would argue that:

'recall' is by no means the only thing we want learners to become able to do if most self-assessment questions asked merely for recall, open learners would quickly get bored with them and skip them; a variety of structured questions helps to make learners' tasks more interesting

in real life, being able to *handle* and *process* information is much more useful than merely being able to recall it from memory; structured questions help learners develop their information handling and processing skills

- more progressive forms of formal assessment are slowly coming to the fore. for example 'open book' exams, where learners have access to all the information they need, and their task is to demonstrate that they can handle it successfully
- all structured questions, in one way or another, lead learners to exercising decision-making skills, and the level of decision-making can be very high if the questions are structured so that they need 'deep thought' before learners commit themselves to an option or a verdict
- where learners 'write' their decisions into spaces or boxes in the open learning materials, they have a permanent record of the way they handled each self-assessment question. This is particularly useful when they made incorrect or 'less good' decisions, which they are thereby alerted to, and can steer clear of in future. It's useful to suggest that *after* learners have tackled a self-assessment question, they can go back to their original answer and amend it with a pen of a different colour, so that they can easily remind themselves later of traps they fell into, and so on.

Filling in blanks

At some levels, this sort of question is ideal. At basic levels, for example, it can allow learners to think about key points without having to worry about grammar, punctuation and all the other things involved in writing full answers. However, because filling-in-blanks questions are useful for situations where learners have perhaps limited skills of literacy, it is possible for more advanced learners to feel patronized. One of the key skills in designing self-assessment questions is to choose appropriate styles and formats, on the basis of your knowledge of the sorts of people who will be learning from your materials. Here's a simple example from chemistry:

SELF-ASSESSMENT QUESTION 4

Complete the following sentences, selecting appropriate words from the list given below:

When any _____ metal is added to dilute _____ acid, a very violent reaction occurs and _____ gas is produced – it will probably catch fire.

If copper, a metal of the _____ type, is added to concentrated _____ acid, _____ gas is produced, which is _____ .

    nitrogen dioxide
    hydrogen
    oxygen
    transition
    alkali
    hydrochloric
    nitric
    brown
    colourless

RESPONSE TO SELF-ASSESSMENT QUESTION 4

The correct answer is as follows:

When any *alkali* metal is added to dilute *hydrochloric* acid, a very violent reaction occurs and *hydrogen* gas is produced – it will probably catch fire.

If copper, a metal of the *transition* type, is added to concentrated *nitric* acid, *nitrogen dioxide* gas is produced, which is *brown*.

Comments:
If you got this completely right, well done. Do check that you got the acids the right way round. Copper doesn't react with hydrochloric acid, whether dilute or concentrated. This is because copper is below hydrogen in the reactivity series. If you put *oxygen* anywhere, beware. I can't think of any metal-acid reaction producing oxygen.

If you said *colourless* instead of *hydrogen* you're quite right in fact – but the name of the product of a reaction is always more important than its colour.

Note once again how I have designed the response so that learners will se something very like the question they answered, with the completed words in th same places as the blanks were. As you've seen from my example, the respons *includes* the correct answer, but should go quite a lot further. Learners who hav made particular mistakes can be helped as directly as possible. At the same time learners who have answered the question correctly should still find usefu reinforcement in the response, helping to ensure that they continue to look a the responses, rather than simply pressing on through the learning materia Filling-in-blanks questions can be made more open-ended by *not* providing a lis of words to choose from, but of course this means that it isn't possible t respond directly to learners who insert a word you haven't dreamt of!

You'll notice in my question I had a couple of extra words as distractors. O course, this type of question need not be confined to words – numbers, symbols labels on diagrams, key points on graphs and so on can equally well be filled ir

Sequencing

This can be a bit of a game for learners. Their task is to place each of several step in the correct order or sequence. First, have a look at this bad example of th genre!

SELF-ASSESSMENT QUESTION 5

Rearrange the following steps into the order in which you should do things when making bread:

(a)   take bread out of oven
(b)   turn on oven
(c)   turn off oven
(d)   weigh out flour
(e)   measure out yeast
(f)   measure out water
(g)   leave in a warm place
(h)   knead the dough
(i)   mix in the water
(j)   add the yeast
(k)   add the flour
(l)   take a bowl
(m)   take out of oven
(n)   put into oven

I'm sure you can see what's wrong with this. Firstly, far too many steps. How many learners would actually check their order against that given in the response? Secondly, of course, there is not *one* correct order in this example. You could make bread by a number of routes containing the listed steps.

So, it's worth adopting a couple of rules for sequencing self-assessment questions:

   make sure that there is one – and only one – correct order of steps
   don't use more than five or six steps at the most.

Doing otherwise makes it difficult to write the response. (I'm not even going to try to write a response to self-assessment question 5!) The response must, of course, include the right answer, but it also needs to explain the most likely errors. If we were to take on board all possible combinations of even five steps, the response would be far too long! That's why responses to sequencing questions should only address the *most likely* errors.

There is a way out of the difficulties of responding to sequencing self-assessment questions. Four or five different sequences can be made the options in a multiple-choice question! Then it's possible to reply about exactly what's wrong with each of the incorrect sequences. However, learners may well find the different sort of activity involved in sequencing questions a welcome change from option picking.

True–False

I'm not too keen on true–false questions in general. After all, the guess-factor is 50 per cent. However, true–false questions have some uses. Suppose, for example, an exact definition is to be learned. A true–false question could pose either the correct definition or one with a deliberate error or omission. The response to the self-assessment question could then deal directly with the error or omission.

When using true–false questions, we need to be particularly careful that 'true' statements are absolutely true. This is sometimes more difficult than it seems! There are so often exceptions to seemingly true statements. We don't want high-fliers choosing the 'false' option because they happen to know an exception to something which was intended to be seen as a 'true' statement.

Despite the disadvantages of true–false questions, they can become rather more useful in clusters. For example, they can serve as a mini-quiz, helping learners to find whether or not they have mastered a number of connected points.

As with other sorts of self-assessment question, it's important that when learners turn to the response, they should see something that looks just like the original question (rather than simply a list of answers or comments). This helps remind them of their thinking as they answered the question and made their decisions about each true–false item. It needs to be quite clear from a glance at the response whether each item is true or false. It would be unhelpful to have a long, rambling explanation which ended '...and therefore it is false to say that...'.

The following example shows some of the possibilities.

SELF-ASSESSMENT QUESTION 6

How much electrical energy do the following domestic appliances use? Decide which of the values below are 'true' or 'false'.

		true	false
Electric kettle	1500 W		
Electric cooker	3000 W		
Electric iron	50 W		
Soldering iron	2 kW		
Hairdryer	80 W		
Light bulb	13 W		
Television	200 W		
Extractor fan	600 W		

Clearly, with this sort of question, it's not possible to do much more than provide an 'answer' rather than a response. However, adding in a few words explaining why the false options are wrong can turn such an answer into something more responsive. I've tried to do this in the response below.

RESPONSE TO SELF-ASSESSMENT QUESTION 6

The wattages of electrical appliances vary quite a lot, but in general the figures given in the question are true or false as follows:

		true	false
Electric kettle	1500 W	✓	
Electric cooker (when using most rings and elements)	3000 W	✓	
Electric iron (this would be very slow indeed!)	50 W		✓
Soldering iron (this would melt more than the solder!)	2 kW		✓
Hairdryer (this would be far too slow)	80 W		✓
Light bulb (but only if it's a low-energy bulb)	13 W	✓	
Television (some portable sets use even less)	200 W	✓	
Extractor fan (unless it's extracting the air from a very large building)	600 W		✓

Completion questions

In one sense, these are really just special cases of the filling-in-blanks type we looked at earlier. Such questions are quite useful in little sets to help test-out several related bits of information. Distractors can be used to reduce 'redundancy'. Of course, such questions could be used without a list of words or terms to choose from, but then it would not be possible to respond directly to what learners may have written. Overleaf is a simple example.

SELF-ASSESSMENT QUESTION 7

Complete each sentence with the correct term from the list given below:

(a)   Current is measured in
(b)   Potential difference is measured in
(c)   Resistance is measured in
(d)   Current multiplied by resistance would have the dimensions of
(e)   Current multiplied by voltage would have the dimensions of

    watts
    ohms
    amps
    volts
    joules

Responses to such questions need to give the correct answer, and some additional comment directed towards learners who make the most likely mistakes. Let's go on to the response to the question above – you may wish to try the question before looking at the response.

RESPONSE TO SELF-ASSESSMENT QUESTION 7

Complete each sentence with the correct term from the list given below:

(a)   Current is measured in *amps*. (Careful not to say 'joules' here; amps are actually 'joules' multiplied by seconds.)

(b)   Potential difference is measured in *volts*. (Of course, there wouldn't have been any doubt if I'd asked what 'voltages' were measured in! 'Potential difference' means the same thing.)

(c)   Resistance is measured in *ohms*. (Remember that Ohm's Law expresses how resistance depends on voltage and current at constant temperature.)

(d)   Current multiplied by resistance would have the dimensions of *volts*. (Again, if you're at home with Ohm's Law, you will get this right.)

(e)   Current multiplied by voltage would have the dimensions of *watts*. (Many people remember this by thinking of the name 'Ivy Watts': I × V = watts.)

Comments: If you got all five of these correct, splendid. If not, have another go at this question tomorrow, and the next day, until you always get it right. Getting the dimensions right will be a very useful skill for you when you go on to Section 2.

Fault finding

This sort of question lends itself particularly well to visual information. It also tends to be a rather attractive thing for learners to do as a change now and then. Learners usually enjoy the game of trying to work out what's wrong with something – especially if the challenge is quantifiable. For example, asking learners to 'Find five things wrong with this diagram' is a more useful challenge than merely 'What's wrong with this diagram' – in the latter case, learners may stop looking for faults after finding the first one.

Such questions give some information, with in-built errors, and ask learners to spot these errors. The technique can be used for all sorts of visual information, for example:

- diagrams (missing bits, extra bits)
- circuit diagrams (wrong components and so on)
- flowcharts (incorrect sequences and so on)
- maps (wrong locations, features)
- pictures (safety hazards, for example).

The briefing is important. For example: 'What's wrong with this circuit diagram?' isn't as good as: 'This circuit wouldn't work: see if you can find three things you would need to alter to get it working'.

Responses can give the correct answer and a short discussion of each of the faults. It's also useful to mention in the response any correct things that learners may have interpreted as faults. Fault-finding questions can also be used with pure text, but this isn't as much fun as with visual information.

Open-ended SAQs

All the types of self-assessment question we've explored so far have been 'closed' to some extent. In other words, there has been some imposed structure, with restrictions on the possible answers. This is excellent in allowing us to *respond* to particular learner mistakes. However, in many disciplines, learners may be heading towards formal exams with open-ended questions. It's easy enough to write open-ended questions. It's even relatively easy to design marking schemes for open-ended exam questions, so that all candidates are fairly assessed. (We'll explore the design of marking schemes in Chapter 6.)

When considering open-ended questions as self-assessment questions, the real issue is how to *respond* to whatever learners may do. The problem is that we don't really know what the learners may have included in their answers.

It's quite easy to write a model answer and use that as part of the response. But that's not really enough. The learners need to know *how* right or *how* wrong parts of their answers were. They may also want to know what their answers would have scored in an exam. Open learners need all the help we can give them about exactly how well or badly they are doing. If using open-ended self-assessment questions, how can we tell them?

Equip learners so they can self-assess their answers

One way is to provide a skeleton model answer *with marking scheme*. Each learner can then go carefully through his or her own answer, finding out just how right or how wrong it was. Of course, the marking scheme needs to be a good one, catering for all reasonable alternatives that learners may have come up with.

When designing marking schemes or checklists to enable learners to self-assess their answers to open-ended questions, remember that learners will not necessarily be accustomed to using marking schemes. Therefore, you will need to make one which is self-explanatory, and which avoids the sort of shortcuts or jargon which creep into examiners' marking schemes.

The cop out?

Another way may be a cop-out but can be very useful: turn the self-assessment question into a question in a tutor-marked assignment! (Many a 'failed' self-assessment question ends up as a question in a tutor-marked assignment!) It's worth thinking about this if the learners really do need a personal assessment and direct comment on their strengths and weaknesses. But then, of course, they no longer have the comfort of making their mistakes in private.

SAQ quality control

When I'm asked to judge the quality of open learning material, the first things I look at are the self-assessment questions, and particularly their responses. If all's well with these, the material is probably excellent.

Composing self-assessment questions and responses is not just a job for authors of open learning materials. Adding new self-assessment questions and responses, and improving existing ones are the most important aspects of modifying existing learning materials to turn them into resources which can be used in open learning.

I set out below a fairly stringent checklist regarding self-assessment questions and responses. I'm not suggesting that every single self-assessment question and response should measure up to each of the criteria I list, but rather that, *cumulatively*, self-assessment questions and responses should live up to the set of criteria.

I've expressed each of my criteria in the form of a question; below each main question I've elaborated, often by spelling-out further questions to pin down what I'm really getting at. Adjusting self-assessment questions and responses so that there is a favourable answer to each of these questions is one way of refining the interactive components of open learning materials.

Quality checklist

Is it really a self-*assessed* question?

How easy is it for any learner *quantitatively* to assess his or her performance? Is the response clear enough to attract the learner to do this rigorously? (For example, if the question involved a calculation containing several successive steps, can any learners who end up with the wrong final answer discover how much credit they deserve for those steps they did correctly?)

How *useful* are the responses?

Do the responses deal with likely learner errors? Do they deal with *all* such errors? Do the responses address learners' needs to know: 'Was I right?' 'If not, why not?'

Does the question involve 'redundancy'?

Are parts of the question automatically got right when other, easier, parts have been completed? Would the use of extra distractors reduce such redundancy? Or is the level of redundancy acceptable?

Does the question actually test something important?

Does the question test the achievement of a reasonably important objective? (It's often all too easy to compose a brilliant self-assessment question about something trivial, and much harder to compose one about something crucial.)

Does the response congratulate learners who got it correct?

Have you avoided being patronizing in your praise? Are different ways of saying well done' used? And does the response remind learners *what* they got right (reinforcement)?

Does the response help learners to feel that their mistakes are reasonable?

Learners who get the self-assessment question wrong may feel that they have just failed something. Is this feeling dealt with humanely? Are learners given the feeling that it is *useful* for them to make mistakes in self-assessment questions, so that they can discover the causes of such mistakes – and cure them?

Does the response put learners back on the right track?

It's of limited use saying 'Read page 3 again'. Learners may make the same mistake again. It's much better to deal with the mistake head-on in the response.

Are both the question and response friendly in tone?

To make questions attractive and motivating, it's best to avoid formality. 'Consider...' is more off-putting than 'Think about...'. (I've included more suggestions on user-friendly language in Chapter 5.)

Is the task quite clear?

It's so easy for instructions to be ambiguous or confusing. When you look at your question, you see what *you meant* to ask. Will your learners read it the same way?

Will learners be tempted to 'cheat' on the question?

Learners working on their own can always choose to look straight to the response. However, this temptation can be reduced, for example, if the question is attractive and motivating. 'Cheating' can also occur if learners can see the answer to the question in the same 'eyeful' as the self-assessment question itself.

Will learners be tempted to skip the question?

This is always a temptation as learners want to press on. However, if the responses are so good that learners become conditioned to being helped by them, the temptation to skip self-assessment questions is reduced considerably.

Does the question give the learner useful practice in things that may be involved later in formal assessment or exams?

Do the self-assessment questions give learners that vital way of making any mistakes with the comfort of privacy?

Have you avoided any sudden jump in standard between one self-assessment question and the next?

An unexpectedly hard self-assessment question can cause the learner to shut the book! Of course, if you say something like 'The next self-assessment question is quite a tough one; take your time with it' learners will accept your challenge.

Are the responses really responses – or just answers?

Learners working on their own need *responses*, not just answers. They need a response to what *they* have done in answer to the question. In other words, they need feedback.

Conclusions

I've gone into considerable detail regarding the role of self-assessment questions and responses because these elements are the main advantage of good open learning materials over simple textbooks or manuals. In open learning, it's the things that open learners *do* that are important – not just the things that they read. When open learners have had a go at a task, they need feedback on what *they* have done – they need more than just correct answers. Now that we've explored two of the principal dimensions of open learning materials (objectives and self-assessment question responses) we can move on to think about how best to go about the task of putting together a piece of open learning material in its entirety.

Chapter 5

Tone and Style for Flexible Learning

Abstract

We've already looked at the design of the most important elements of open learning materials: namely, details of the intended learning outcomes, and self-assessment questions and responses. My intention in this chapter is to help you organize the remaining parts of the task of writing open learning material, including some comments on the sort of language that may work best when it comes to composing text to join one self-assessment question's response to the next question. In this chapter, I'll also mention briefly the use of visual material, using non-print media, and presentation of material. If you are more likely to be adapting existing materials rather than composing new ones from scratch, I think you'll find the suggestions in this chapter equally helpful.

Objectives

When you've explored this chapter, you should feel more confident regarding:

- writing in a relatively informal, user-friendly style
- choosing an efficient, systematic way of putting together the principal components of open learning material
- making sure that open learners can get the most out of any visual material you include (graphs, diagrams, tables, charts, pictures and so on)
- ensuring that any non-print media you employ are serving learners as effectively as possible
- using presentation or 'house style' aspects to enhance the learning experiences of users of open learning materials you develop.

User-friendly tone and style

In writing open learning materials, or composing modifications (such as additional self-assessment questions and responses) to existing ones, many people now agree that an easy-to-read, informal tone is best – especially for learners who are working by themselves for much of their time. If you're already well practised in writing things in an easy-to-read, lively, informal style, then this chapter will hold few surprises for you.

Of course, not everyone agrees with the use of informal, friendly language. If you're one of these people, this chapter is aimed at you! Not everyone finds it easy to write that way – even if most of us *speak* that way most of the time even when teaching!

Why make a special effort to write in user-friendly language?

For many people it does require a special effort at first. One of the reasons for this can be traced back to our schooldays. Can you remember being encouraged to write in ever more complex language? Teachers were pleased with us when we first mastered the art of stringing together longer sentences, with more clauses and longer words (especially if we were able to spell the longer words too). It did not stop at school, however. You have probably noticed that as our lives develop, we often need to write in more complex language in reports, memos, proposals and so on. If we write in simple, basic language, there seems to be a danger that our messages will not be taken seriously. Yet it is said that if you choose your words carefully, you can explain something as complicated as the theory of relativity to a seven-year-old, using short sentences and simple words and models.

Indeed, my argument is that the use of long words and long sentences becomes elitist. Such language can exclude many people from understanding our messages. Some people are happy with such exclusion, but if you're in the business of getting your ideas across to learners, there's little place for additional barriers of this sort.

In the self-assessment question below, I quote several things that people say about informal, user-friendly language – some approving and others critical. Please decide whether you agree or disagree with each statement, then turn to my response on page 129, where I give my reaction to each point of view.

SELF-ASSESSMENT QUESTION 5.1

The arguments for and against informal tone and style

Decide whether you agree or disagree with each of the 12 statements below, then compare your views with mine, given in my responsee on page 129.

1   Using informal, user-friendly language will help make open learners working on their own feel welcome and at ease.
2   Using informal, user-friendly language will make it easier to learn – even with advanced subject material.
3   Using informal, user-friendly language will insult and patronize most learners.
4   Using informal, user-friendly language wil damage your credibility as an author or a teacher.
5   Using informal, user-friendly language will extend learning opportunities to learners of limited language skills (such as students for whom English is a second language).
6   Using informal, user-friendly language will help your learners to become better at communicating in writing.
7   Using informal, user-friendly language will cause your learners to develop bad habits in their use of language.
8   Using informal, user-friendly language will assist 'low-fliers' to concentrate on the topic, unhindered by the language.
9   Using informal, user-friendly language will irritate high-fliers.
10 Using informal, user-friendly language will allow high-fliers to learn even more rapidly.
11 Using informal, user-friendly language is an art which I will not attempt to master!
12 Using informal, user-friendly language will be a major aim of mine in writing self-study materials.

(Remember to check your decisions against my opinions – see the response on page 129.)

Can you *measure* your tone and style?

One of the most frequently used (and abused!) devices for measuring readability is the Modified Fog Index. This has been widely criticized, and it is indeed a blunt instrument. However, it is a start – and it most certainly can tell you things about the level at which you are writing. The Modified Fog Index scores the 'reading age' of a piece of writing. If you score, say, 20, it means something like this:

- people whose reading age is less than 20 will have considerable difficulty understanding your writing: they may have to read it several times before they get your meaning
- people with a reading age above 20 should be able to understand your writing more easily.

Calculating Modified Fog Index

So, how do you find your Modified Fog Index? Take a chunk of something you've written. Alternatively, take a chunk of something somebody else has written. Now go through the following operations.

1   Bracket off a sample of exactly 100 words. Sorry, this does mean counting them. Start at the beginning of a sentence, but don't worry if you end up in the middle of a sentence.
2   Underline each word that has three or more syllables. If such a word occurs several times, underline it each time. Then count the number of words you've underlined. This gives you 'L'. L = number of long words.
3   Count the number of sentences. Round it up or down to the nearest whole number.
4   Work out the average number of words per sentence by dividing 100 by your number of sentences and rounding the answer up or down to the nearest whole number. This gives you 'A'. A = average words per sentence.
5   Add A to L.
6   Multiply (A + L) by 4.
7   Divide by 10.
8   Add 5.

The result is the reading age of your chosen piece. Of course, if you're mathematically minded, you'll prefer to use a formula rather than the list of steps above.

The formula is: reading age $= ((A + L) \times 4/10) + 5$

How did you score? It's reckoned that a score of 20 or more means that the text is for the highly literate only. If you're in doubt, try the test on newspaper stories. Even the more upmarket ones rarely score more than 15. Some tabloids communicate at under 10! Think what newspaper your learner would be most likely to read on a train – and measure its Modified Fog Index.

How can you get your Fog Index down?

I'm assuming you want it down! Of course, you may be thinking of applying for certain Civil Service senior posts where the thing to do is to use such complicated linguistic skills that only the highly educated and persistent reader can untangle the matrix of adjectival, adverbial and other clauses, yet still discover the subject, object and verb in each of your long, flowing sentences! Made my point?

There are two simple ways of improving your readability, each bringing the Modified Fog Index down. A combination of both works best: use fewer long words; make sentences shorter. I set out below some phrases which can often be replaced by a single word and some multi-syllable words which can often be replaced by a shorter one. Of course, I don't claim the substitution is perfect in all cases.

Longer phrase	Shorter version
establish a connection between	link
paying appropriate attention to	noting
in the immediate vicinity of	near
attain a consensus decision	agree
under no circumstances whatsoever	never
at every available opportunity	whenever
without the slightest reservation	definitely
arrive at the conclusion	conclude
reach the decision	decide
it may well turn out to be that	probably
with a fair degree of probability	probably
maintained in a perpendicular alignment	held upright
unable to proceed further	stuck
aligned in a horizontal position	lying flat
socially withdrawn and inhibited	shy
at the present moment in time	now
on a subsequent occasion	next time
render assistance to	help
ascertain the exact location of	find
in a stationary state	stopped
in the eventuality of	if
in the absence of	without

Using single words or short phrases instead of lengthy phrases can obviously help to reduce Fog Index. A further process can be used to get it even lower – 'delatinizing' your English. Many words in the English language have Latin roots, and many such words tend to be multi-syllabic. Words of Anglo-Saxon origin are often shorter and more direct. Curiously, most people use more Anglo-Saxon words when they talk than when they write. The following table shows some examples of this.

Longer word	Shorter word(s)
unprecedented	new
advantageous	useful
beneficial	good
disadvantage	snag
commencement	start
consequently	so
deficiency	lack of
excessive	too much
inadequate	not enough
facilitate	help
subsequently	later
utilization	use
expenditure	cost
fundamental	basic
furthermore	and
illustrate	show
considerable	much
substantial	big
necessitate	need
speculation	guess
predominant	main

In a series of items separated by commas, you can improve readability by setting the items out as a list, as is done often in this book. If you did the Modified Fog Index calculation a little earlier, now's your chance to look back at the words you underlined. Some of them may have been quite necessary. But how many could you now replace with a word of one or two syllables? This can bring the Fog Index down – and the readability up.

'Action' language

Now I'd like you to think about writing in the first person and addressing your reader directly. The traditional textbook tends to rely on the third-person passive tense. So it might write up an observation in the chemistry laboratory like this:

It can be observed that when copper nitrate is incinerated in a test-tube, an emanation of brown fumes is produced, having a characteristic noxious odour.

But how much more involving this passage would be if it read like this:

> If you take some copper nitrate and heat it in a test-tube, you'll see brown fumes evolved, and you'll notice an unpleasant smell. Have you tried this yet?

Words like 'you', 'I' and 'we' make the reader feel involved. They make the writer seem more like a fellow human being. The question at the end of the above example is also there to make learners feel more active. Questions make one think.

Stitching the bits together

The open learning writer needs to be a Jack or Jill of many trades. It's not just a case of telling a story, the module needs to be something that causes learning to occur. It also matters *how* the learning occurs. The aim should be for it to occur efficiently, enjoyably, lastingly and actively. My purpose in this chapter is to make it easier for you to organize and structure your tasks as you put together open learning material.

Let me first try to scare you by pointing out just how many different considerations you're likely to be dealing with! A good open learning module doesn't just contain printed pages which look more or less alike, it contains various tools to help the learning process take place. The previous two chapters looked at some of these tools. The components in any good open learning module include most of the following:

- learning outcomes (see Chapter 3)
- self-assessment questions and responses (see Chapter 4)
- text, introductions, reviews, summaries (discussed in the present chapter)
- visual information (this chapter): diagrams, graphs, charts, tables, pictures, even cartoons perhaps
- assignments (see Chapters 6 and 7) for tutor or computer marking.

Other things you are likely to be involved with include:

- explanation of prerequisite knowledge/skills
- 'house style' page layout, use of white space, structure of the material
- signposting: reminding learners where they're heading; showing learners when they've got there!

You may need to think carefully about exactly who the learners will be. You may have additional complications, such as referred reading in textbooks, journals and so on. There may be practical work to design and explain. There may even be a home 'kit' to design and produce. There may also be components such as video tapes, audio tapes and other non-print media. Once the material is beginning to take shape, you may need to assume an editor's role, looking at it objectively and dispassionately.

You'll also be involved in testing out your material, and making numerous adjustments to it in the light of experience – mainly the experience of your learners. Now are you beginning to see that it's not going to be possible simply to sit down with pen and paper and start? It's unwise to begin writing without a fair bit of planning first.

In Chapter 2, I suggested a general strategy for writing open learning materials based on starting with the intended learning outcomes (or objectives), developing from these the self-assessment questions and responses, and linking one response to the next question by adding text 'bridges'. At the same time, I suggested that where it is not easily possible to build-in structured feedback into the learning materials themselves (ie, where human judgment and feedback is needed by learners), it's useful to be developing tutor-marked assignment questions alongside.

A problem in writing open learning materials is that most authors have the 'content' on their minds, and this interferes with their efforts to turn it into learner actions and feedback. It's instinctive to want to write down the facts, theories, concepts, discussions and so on: some people do not really feel they have started to write anything until they have got such things down on paper.

However, with open learning materials, much of the content need not be written in the 'text' as such at all, but can be saved for inclusion in the feedback responses which follow self-assessment questions or activities. After all, some learners may know much of the 'content' already – they only need to read it if they need to refresh their knowledge, for example when they cannot quite manage an activity or self-assessment question. For those learners who don't know any particular piece of content, they find out in due course after trying a self-assessment question and getting a wrong answer or not being able to complete it. What's more, they are alerted to the fact that they did not know the piece of content concerned. (Simply *reading* through the content in textbooks, for example, does not really alert one to which bits of it one doesn't yet know properly.)

One of the primary benefits of the strategy I have suggested is that devices such as self-assessment questions and responses are not just 'add-ons' but an integral part of the way the material is built. This means that any learners who simply try to 'read' the learning materials are constantly reminded that this is not the way the materials work.

When can I write some 'text'?

Of course you *can* write it at any time, but I'm suggesting that various other things are best done first. The advantage of having things such as self-assessment questions and responses already composed is that you know exactly where each element of text is leading from – and to. In other words, your task of text-writing is much better defined. So *which* bit of text is it best to start with?

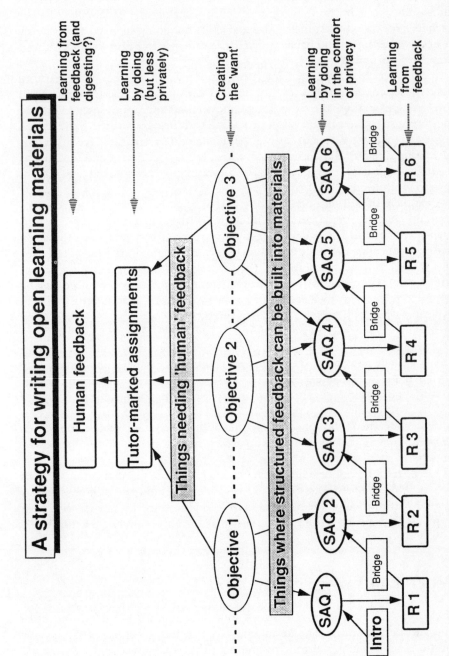

A strategy for writing open learning materials

Learning from feedback (and digesting?)

Learning by doing (but less privately)

Creating the 'want'

Learning by doing in the comfort of privacy

Learning from feedback

Human feedback

Tutor-marked assignments

Things needing 'human' feedback

Objective 1   Objective 2   Objective 3

Things where structured feedback can be built into materials

Intro — SAQ 1 — Bridge — R 1

SAQ 2 — Bridge — R 2

SAQ 3 — Bridge — R 3

SAQ 4 — Bridge — R 4

SAQ 5 — Bridge — R 5

SAQ 6 — Bridge — R 6

Figure 5.1   A reminder of the strategy proposed in Chapter 2.

Starting at the beginning?

The first bit of text is a very important one. It needs to have the right effect on learners. What should it be like?

Friendly

If the initial text is formal or remote, learners may well feel that they aren't really going to be any more involved in the learning than they are with an ordinary textbook. So words such as 'you' (the learner) and 'I' (the author) are needed to start off in user-friendly manner.

Motivating

If the introduction is boring, learners may well close the module without ever getting started! If the introduction is stimulating, learners are much more likely to press on and get involved.

Short

There's nothing more daunting to open learners than a double-page eyeful of unbroken text! That *looks* like a lot of hard work. So it's best to make the introduction as short as possible, then get straight into some form of activity – for example, a self-assessment question. You don't have to wait until they've learned something to pose the first self-assessment question. You can ask something along these lines, even on page 1:

> 'What do you think the most likely causes of . . . are? If you don't yet know, just have a guess for now. See if you can think of three – then we'll go on to explore the causes in detail.'

The introduction

There's no second chance to make a good first impression. Learners will base their entire view of an open learning package on the first few paragraphs they encounter. One of the key purposes of the very first part of a package is to whet learners' appetites – in other words, to create the 'want' to learn from the package. Do you think it's best to write the introduction:

- before writing the text of the section, and its self-assessment question and responses?
- after the text has been written, but before writing the self-assessment questions and responses?
- after the text, self-assessment questions and responses have been drafted out?

The best position to be in when you write the introduction is that represented by the last of the above – that is, when you know exactly what you're introducing.

Reviews, summaries, checklists

The best open learning materials always remind the learner of just what has been learned. Simply repeating the main points is much better than just stopping at the end of a piece of material. However, it's much better to make the review or summary something *active* for learners. That's where checklists can come into their own. In fact, it should be quite easy to write a checklist for any well-designed piece of open learning material. The objectives should lie at the centre of such a checklist. For example:

> Now that you've completed section Z, check that you feel confident to:
> (a)
> (b)

The main advantage of having a suitable review, summary or checklist is that you get the main ideas one more time through each learner's mind. Successful learning is very much to do with how many times something has been thought about. Reflection – or 'digesting' as I prefer to call it – is a vital part of the learning process.

I'd like now to explore three other dimensions of writing open learning materials: visual material, choosing and using non-print media, and signposting. These may not be quite so central to writing strategy as some of the things we've already looked at, but they're all very important as far as your learners are concerned. And, in practice, the sooner you start thinking about all of these things, the easier it is to ensure that they all contribute effectively to the quality of the material you produce.

Visual material

Most people find that visual images are more memorable than words alone. One of the principal differences between a conventional textbook and good open learning material is that the latter is usually more visually stimulating. Indeed, when learners come across a double-page spread of pure print, it can seem like a good time to put the book down! However, it's not enough to have plenty of visual impact – the visual components need to be serving a purpose for the learner. Visual components may include:

- diagrams
- charts
- maps
- tables of data

- graphs
- sketches
- photographs
- cartoons.

Some of the features of open learning materials can be 'visual' in their own right, including:

- boxes to tick, or giving space to fill in answers to questions
- lists of 'bullet points' (like this one), making things stand out better than they would have in continuous prose
- self-assessment questions and activities, maybe with 'icons' to signal them
- headings and subheadings, giving an at-a-glance map of the material in sight at any moment.

Let's work through a checklist of questions. It's worth having these questions at the back of your mind all the time you're putting together open learning material.

Can I make it 'visual'?

An illustration, it is said, can be worth a thousand words. A good one can certainly save you time and trouble while writing. Or it can help make sure your learners get the right message from your words. Or it can show them an idea from another point of view. The flowchart I drew to explain my suggestions for the most logical strategy for putting together open learning materials is (I think) much easier to latch on to than if I simply tried to explain it all in words (as I did in the first edition of this book!).

To what standard should it be drawn?

You may be no artist: it doesn't matter. For example, if you want your learners to become able to sketch a grommit, there's not much point having a cross-section of a grommit drawn by a professional graphics designer shown in your material. Your learners wouldn't identify with that. What they need is a *sketch*, and yours would probably be as good as anyone's.

Do the learners know what to do with it?

Whatever kind of illustration you are using, you must be sure that your learners know what to do with it. They could, for instance, be expected to:

- do nothing except notice it in passing
- sketch it freehand
- reproduce it exactly, to scale
- remember all the numbers in a table
- pick out the trends from a table (but not remember numbers)

- interpret the data in a table or the shape of a graph
- recognize it again next time they see it
- write labels on a similar diagram.

It only takes a few words of guidance to make the learners' task clear. Those few words can save learners trying to learn things you don't intend them to learn and make sure they do learn what you want them to learn. In face-to-face sessions, learners often ask for clarification regarding diagrams, tables, graphs and so on. 'Do we have to remember this?' is a common question. Our answers to this question are useful to them. A few words in brackets after the caption can give open learners this valuable information, for example:

(You only need to be able to pick out the trends.)
(You need to be able to sketch graphs like Fig.3.)
(This diagram is simply to show you how a grommit in linked to the other parts of the dobulator.)
(You could be asked to draw and label a cross-section like Fig. 5.)
(Don't worry, you don't have to draw one of these!)

Choosing and using non-print media

Many open learning packages consist of printed materials and nothing else. We've already looked at ways of presenting material in non-textbook style. The heart of open learning is the interaction between the learner working alone and the material. Of course, it is possible to design open learning materials using media other than print, such as:

- video tape (most people have some access to domestic video equipment)
- audio tape (almost everyone has a 'Walkman')
- tape/slide (usually for use in a training centre or resources centre)
- filmstrip and viewer (maybe with an audio commentary too)
- computer-based material
- interactive video
- interactive audio
- CD-I (interactive compact disc)
- practical kits.

and various combinations of such media. (For a detailed discussion, see Ellington and Race (1993) in the Bibliography.)

It is not my purpose here to go through all the pros and cons of each of these media. Nor is it my purpose to suggest which of these it may be best for you to use. However, I would like to arm you with a critical checklist to help you make appropriate choices.

Above all, I'd like to help you make sure that any non-print media you decide to use are employed *actively* rather than as optional add-on material. For example, carefully prepared videotapes often accompany open learning pack ages, but do the producers realize how *passively* we are conditioned to watch the small screen? Do they realize how little of what we see and hear we remember after a few days? Have they noticed that when we watch a video recording for a second time, we usually notice all sorts of things that we didn't notice the first time round? Learners may just watch the video once unless carefully advised otherwise.

Furthermore, we need to think about how best learners' approaches to media-based components of their learning packages can be structured. If they know what they're intended to be getting out of the media elements, there's much more chance they will be successful.

The checklist below should be equally useful if you're thinking about designing some media-based support for existing learning materials or examining the effectiveness of existing media-backed open learning materials with a view to making improvements where necessary.

Checklist for medium X

Let's suppose you've decided to use medium X as part of an open learning package you are creating (where X can be anything from interactive video to simple audio tapes). You should have good answers to each of the following questions.

Why is X better than print alone?

There should be good answers to justify using X. For example, video can be justified where learners need to see things moving, or to see things they could not see directly (such as the inside of a working nuclear reactor), or to experience the tensions and subtleties of live human interaction such as drama, debates and so on. Alternatively, X can be used as an introduction to a learning package where the main intention of using X is to 'create the want' – to whet learners' appetite for the package as a whole.

What will learners do with X?

For example, if a 15-minute video is to be used, it's not much good if learners just sit back and watch. We all forget most of what we see on a television screen. Your learners need to have definite things to be got out of watching the video. For example, learners could have five questions to answer while watching the video. If such questions are already planted firmly in their minds before starting to view the video, the viewing becomes much more active. Alternatively, learners could be asked to answer certain questions after watching the video to show them whether the important parts of the message have got across. A video accompanied by a workbook is likely to be more successful than a video alone. The same arguments apply to many varieties of X.

What learning outcomes does the use of X lead towards?

It's all too easy to get carried away and stray on to matters that aren't included in the original objectives of the open learning material. Having made sure that the material in medium X does relate to the learning objectives or competences, it's necessary to explain to learners exactly which objectives or competences are involved. In other words, learners need to know exactly what X is helping them to achieve. Coupling the use of X to self-assessment questions, activities, or tutor-marked assignments can help learners to see that X is not just icing on the cake but an integral part of their learning programme.

Produce X from scratch or adapt?

Particularly with video, the time and expertise needed to produce new material from scratch are usually underestimated. One problem is that we are all used to a very high standard of visual presentation on television. This means that as soon as we see something that is even slightly amateurish, we switch off from the message. It's often possible to start with material of high quality which already exists. It may be necessary to edit, selecting those parts which are directly relevant to the learning objectives and cutting out things that are tangential. It will be necessary to negotiate with the owner of the existing material, but this is often much easier than you may think. Similar considerations apply to other varieties of X.

How easy will it be for the learner to use X?

With audio tape, for example, we can safely assume that just about every learner has easy access to some form of playback. In fact, if audio tapes are a central part of your learning package, it may be worth including the price of a personal stereo in the overall cost of the package. Alternatively, it may be possible to hire out suitable playback equipment on request.

With video, on the other hand, not everyone has access to playback at home. (And access isn't always easy – the rest of the family may have priority demands!) Also, if learners are working on the material well away from video playback facilities, it's not very satisfactory for them to have to stop suddenly and be unable to proceed until they can get access to facilities. So it's necessary to flag well in advance when video playback will be needed.

How early should I compose the X material?

Now we're getting back to basic strategy again. In fact, it's best to start work on any media components right from the outset. It's best to have explored the use that you'll make of such media components right back at the 'objectives' stage of planning your material. However, I didn't bring this dimension in at the outset for two reasons:

if you *start* with the media components, there's the danger that they'll take up all your time, and the writing of the main part of the material may get very rushed

when making audio tapes or video tapes, the first stage is usually a *writing* one in any case – you've got to have a good written script before you're in a position to generate good audio or visual material.

Signposting

It is beyond the scope of this chapter to go into all the aspects of style which have to be taken into account in designing open learning materials. Many such aspects are the responsibility of editors, publishers and printers rather than authors. However, the author can make valuable suggestions regarding the final appearance and structure of the learning materials.

One aspect that should be of particular concern to you, the author, is 'signposting'. This is to do with helping the learners know where they're at, where they're going – and where they've come from! It's about helping them find their way backwards and forwards through the materials. It's perfectly possible to add the signposting at a late stage in writing and production. However, there are advantages in authors being aware of some of the possibilities even before putting pen to paper.

One of the best ways to find out what sorts of signposting you wish to use is to look at as many different samples of open learning materials as you can lay your hands on. Look for things which genuinely seem to help learners find out 'where they are' – and look also for things that seem irritating, distracting and unhelpful. There is no one 'best' way to lay out open learning materials. All sorts of factors must be taken into account, including:

the level of the material
the sorts of people who will be using it
the cost of the materials
the facilities available for final printing and production.

I'd like to list a number of things that you can do to help your learners navigate their way through your materials. First, let's explore some things where you as an author are in complete control.

Author-controlled signposting

Words

Simple bits of explanation can be of great use to learners. For example:

'Now that you've seen how . . . , let's go on to have a look at the effects of . . .'
'For this next part, you'll need to remember what we said about . . . and you'll also need your . . . to hand.'

■ 'We'll soon be exploring why ... happens. First, however, we need to thinl about ...'

Flags

These are the small visual symbols used in many open learning materials to mak various features stand out. Flags can be used for things like:

■ prerequisites (things you should already know)
■ objectives
■ self-assessment questions (for example, a large question mark)
■ responses to self-assessment questions
■ activities
■ practical work
■ pause time (for example, a cup of coffee)
■ stop and reflect
■ review or summary
■ key point
■ useful study tip
■ suitable stopping place
■ tutor-marked assignment (for example, an envelope or pen).

But don't go overboard on flags. If there are more than about half a doze symbols on a page, learners may soon get the meanings confused. It may not b your job as an author to design the flags; however, there's nobody better a making sure that the flags get put in the right places.

Headings

Headings can be really helpful to open learners. Using plenty of headings help break down the material into manageable chunks.

A glance through several headings on a double-page spread can alert th learner to what's to come. Question headings (you may have noticed I use thes quite a lot!) can be particularly useful. Planting questions in the minds c learners creates a sort of thirst for the answers. This means that learners are the more receptive as they work through the materials. Question headings (lik objectives and other expressions of intended learning outcomes) can play useful role in alerting learners to what they should be trying to get out of th materials they study.

'Every fact is simply the answer to a question'. When learners know what th questions are, the facts mean more to them.

Numbers

All sorts of things may need to be numbered so that you can refer learnei backwards and forwards through the materials. You'll often want to ref learners to particular self-assessment questions, responses, diagrams, table activities, assignments, pages, sections and so on. So should headings an paragraphs be numbered too? Personally, I find a lot of numbering is off-putting and formal. I don't like to see Section 1, sub-section 1.2, and sub-sub-section 1.2.4 and so on. You can often use headings instead of numbers. For example, you could ask learners to 'have another look at "How a Grommit Works" on page 12'.

Objectives or competence descriptors

Learning outcomes descriptors serve many purposes (as you'll have seen from Chapter 3). They can help with signposting too. Where they're presented at the start of a section, they tell learners a good deal regarding what the section is going to be about. When they are listed towards the close of a section, they provide learners with a means of checking whether their learning has been successful.

Author-suggested signposting

Here, I'm thinking of other signposting features which may be more the responsibility of the editor, graphics designer, publisher or printer but on which you are in a very strong position to advise.

Boxing

Let's take an example. When your learners come to a self-assessment question, they need to know where it stops! Putting the self-assessment question in some sort of box is one way of making it quite clear where the self-assessment question starts and ends. Boxes may be used to make key points stand out. They can also be used for activities, assignments and so on. It's important not to cause confusion, however: use different kinds of boxes for different things. Different thicknesses of line (or different colours) can make it easy for learners to recognize exactly what sort of information is in each box.

However, beware! For obvious reasons, it's important that the box ends up of approximately the right size in the final printed materials. If learners see a question which requires only a few words to answer, and there is a large box to write it in, they naturally become confused. Even worse, try putting a long answer in a tiny box!

Typefaces

It's well worth authors knowing what typefaces are available to them, and making full use of the range. They may be able to use different sizes of type, bold type and a variety of styles, including italic. By using these carefully, it is easy to distinguish a main heading from a subheading and so on.

Print size and density can also provide ways of distinguishing 'need-to-know' material from 'nice-to-know' material. Important points can be made to stand out visually on the page.

A simple way for authors to let typesetters or publishers know what print size, density or fount is intended is to use colour-coded underlines on draft material, with a key to explain which colour means what. But, of course, colours will be lost in any photocopying – so margin explanations may be safer!

A few suggestions:

DON'T WRITE EXTENDED THINGS IN CAPITAL LETTERS – THEY'RE MUCH HARDER TO READ THAN LOWER-CASE PRINT.

EVEN WORSE, DON'T USE UNDERLINING TOO MUCH. THE ODD WORD IS ALL RIGHT, BUT WHOLE LINES AREN'T!

Small bold phrases stand out well from ordinary text.

A bold heading in lower case
stands out more clearly than the same heading in upper case.

Italics stand out well in founts of the 'Times' variety,
but they *don't* necessarily stand out as well in 'sans serif' founts such as 'Helvetica'.

Unusual founts can add variety and interest to your materials, but check that they are going to be available to you in the final version!

And **finally,** don't get carried away, just because you have several founts *and styles* available to you – this can get **really** irritating!

Indenting

This is another simple, useful way of indicating a subsection or perhaps a self assessment question. Like all signposting devices, indentation becomes annoying to learners if it is used in too complex a way. Have you come across documents where, at the sixth level of indentation, the line of print is only a few centimetres long?!

Colour

It costs a lot to print more than one colour, unfortunately. However, if you've got different colours available to you, it's well worth making use of them. For example, self-assessment questions could be printed in a different colour to mainstream text. It's often possible to use coloured paper for things like self assessment question responses, assignment sheets, glossaries and so on. This can make it easier for learners to locate them. Coloured paper may be quite inexpensive – much less than coloured printing. Whether or not you can easily use coloured pages does, however, depend on the way the material is to be bound.

Size of visuals

I'm thinking here about diagrams, sketches, graphs, charts and so on. The best size for these things depends on what you want learners to do with them. For example, if you want learners to become able to sketch something, it's not much good having a tiny diagram in the learning materials.

If you leave it to other people to decide on the size of visuals, you may be disappointed. They may be more concerned with fitting the various elements on the page than with the sense and structure of the material. It's well worth indicating to the designer, publisher or typesetter your intentions for each visual element in the material.

It's also useful for you, as the author, to state quite clearly *where* each visual should appear. For example, you'll often want certain bits of text to be in sight along with a diagram or chart. (It's very annoying to learners if they have to keep turning back or forward a page.) Publishers unaccustomed to producing open learning materials often seem to have little sense of where illustrations and tables should best appear, and it's worth checking carefully at proof stage that the learners' interests are being served well by the positioning of illustrations. (Also, double-check your captions!)

White space

There are all sorts of uses for white space, including:

- space for learners to write in answers
- space for learners to make additional notes
- space to make important things stand out.

White space is one of the things that makes good open learning materials very different from traditional textbooks. Whenever your learners fill in words, numbers or sketches, they are putting a little of themselves into the materials. This helps them gain some 'ownership' of the materials. Learners have a different sort of regard for materials they've written on. The materials become quite different from an ordinary source of reference.

Somehow, white space seems to get 'reduced' from author's draft to published version – particularly of course where the draft is A4 and the published version is A5. It can be well worth specifying in centimetres how much white space learners will need for their answers to self-assessment questions.

When pressing for white space, you may find yourself being reminded of the cost of paper. However, white space costs very little in fact – it costs nothing to write (though typesetters seem to charge the same per page – whether blank or inky!). Ultimately, the quality of learning that your learners derive, plus their sense of ownership of the materials they write on, can be your defence for using quite a lot of white space in open learning materials.

Page turns

Have you noticed how irritating it is if a major heading comes near the bottom of a right-hand page? It's equally irritating if a list is broken by a page turn. With learning materials, it's very helpful if each self-contained chunk (paragraph, self-assessment question, response, table, list and so on) can be seen in its entirety. Better still, try to arrange it so that most pages begin with a heading or sub-heading. Does it matter if the previous page had a little blank space at the bottom? Sadly, if your publisher has not had some experience in producing open learning materials, you may find yourself constantly having to give reminders that you want new pages to start with new headings whenever this is realistically possible.

Conclusions

In this chapter, we've explored a bewildering number of aspects of the elements which make up a good open learning package. I hope you're not feeling like abandoning your intentions to write (or adapt) open learning material!

I hope that this chapter has given you some thoughts about how best to set about the various tasks involved. You'll have gathered that it's very much a matter of concentrating on one thing at a time, but always with your eye on exactly how that bit is going to fit into the overall product, and how it's eventually going to look. It's a good idea to get your hands on a range of different kinds of open learning material. Look at the different styles. Look for strengths – the things that make the materials work – and emulate them as you write your own material. Also, look out for weaknesses in existing materials, and find ways of avoiding them in your own writing.

The real joy of writing open learning materials comes when you see your learners successfully learning from them. The challenge is not simply to communicate what you know but to structure the materials so that learning from them is efficient, effective and enjoyable. You've probably come to your own conclusions regarding tone and style by now. You'll have noticed that throughout this book I've been trying to write in the sort of informal style I'm advocating. I'm trying to give you a taste of what it feels like to work as an open learner.

Response to self-assessment question 5.1

The arguments for and against informal tone and style

I've repeated the 12 statements I used in the self-assessment question, this time adding my own view about each. Please compare your views with mine.

1   *Using informal, user-friendly language will help make open learners working on their own feel welcome and at ease.*
    I agree. Many open learners have sad memories of their earlier education. Many have felt patronized and insulted by teachers. Many have felt that ego-trips were taken at their expense. Friendly, simple language can make all the difference to winning their commitment. Friendly language compensates for much of the loneliness of the learner working alone.

2   *Using informal, user-friendly language will make it easier to learn – even with advanced subject material.*
    Yes, I agree. Advanced subjects may necessarily involve some complex terminology. That doesn't mean sentences have to be long. It doesn't mean the tone has to be remote and formal. You can write *about* complex things in a friendly, chatty style. That way the learner will think you're a friend and ally, not just a teacher.

3   *Using informal, user-friendly language will insult and patronize most learners.*
    I disagree. The only people who tend to be insulted by simple language in learning material seem to be academics! I believe this is evidence of elitism in our ranks! Do we wish to use language so as to *exclude* less able people?

4   *Using informal, user-friendly language will damage your credibility as an author or a teacher.*
    I disagree. If you were to publish a paper in an academic journal, informal language might cause surprise. However, writing self-study materials is a very different business. In fact, it is likely to enhance your credibility in your subject if you are able to communicate it clearly and fluently. Using informal, user-friendly language will enhance your credibility as a teacher. You'll still be able to use more sophisticated language in papers you submit to prestigious journals if you wish.

5   *Using informal, user-friendly language will extend learning opportunities to learners of limited language skills (such as students for whom English is a second language).*
    I agree. Many students have language problems – not just those learning in a second language. On average, teachers' language skills are more highly developed than those of learners. Language should not be a hurdle. Unless it is a definite objective of your syllabus to develop your learners' language skills, you would do better to concentrate on the real objectives of teaching the subject.

6   *Using informal, user-friendly language will help your learners to become bette*
    at communicating in writing.
    I agree. Many open learners need to develop their written communication
    skills. The more clearly they can express themselves, the better they will do
    in exams. They learn language from example. If learning materials are stiff
    and starchy, learners' writing styles are likely to be the same. When learning
    materials are clear and simple in tone, learners are more likely to become
    able to express themselves easily and fluently.

7   *Using informal, user-friendly language will cause your learners to develop bad*
    habits in their use of language.
    I disagree. Informal, user-friendly writing doesn't have to be grammatically
    bad. It only needs to be simple. There's nothing wrong with short
    sentences. There's nothing wrong with using short words rather than long
    ones – provided the meaning is clear. There's nothing wrong with writing
    as one would speak, especially when communicating through teaching
    materials. Even the opponents of user-friendly style usually *talk* in an
    informal tone. If in doubt, take a few recordings of yourself talking to
    people! The art of writing in an informal, user-friendly style is simply the art
    of writing as you would talk.

8   *Using informal, user-friendly language will assist 'low-fliers' to concentrate on*
    the topic, unhindered by the language.
    I agree. 'Low-fliers' need to be thinking about the subject matter – not
    wasting energy sorting out the language as well. When learning from self-
    study materials, such learners don't have tone of voice to help them sort out
    the meaning of a sentence. The printed words need to communicate as
    clearly as they can.

9   *Using informal, user-friendly language will irritate high-fliers.*
    I don't think so. It seems in fact that even very capable students do not find
    user-friendly language annoying at all. Using simple language is not
    patronizing. If materials are easy to read, high-fliers simply read them
    rather faster. Freedom of pace is surely desirable in open learning.

10 *Using informal, user-friendly language will allow high-fliers to learn even more*
    rapidly.
    This seems to be true. Simple language means that the high-fliers can go
    through the materials all the more rapidly. They can forge ahead until they
    come to something that stretches them a little more.

11 *Using informal, user-friendly language is an art which I will not attempt to*
    master!
    If this is your decision, my advice would be to stay away from writing self-
    study materials! But why not master the art? It's not as if you will be unable
    thereafter to use more sophisticated language. If you master the art of user-
    friendly writing, it's another tool in your toolkit. You may be surprised at
    how often such a tool proves useful. You may even be tempted into
    journalism – where simple language is much respected!

12 *Using informal, user-friendly language will be a major aim of mine in writing self-study materials.*

If you agree with this aim, I'm glad! It's not as hard as it may seem at first. Keep sentences short. When a long word can be replaced by a short one, do so. Keep it friendly. Address your reader as 'you', not 'the learner' or 'the student'. Refer to yourself – the author – as 'I'. Keep in mind the way you *talk* to students.

Chapter 6

Tutor-marked Assignments

Abstract

There are all sorts of 'assignments' used with open learning programmes and in college courses where certain parts of a syllabus are covered by open learning provision. The most usual kind is the tutor-marked assignment (known by most learners as the TMA).

Objectives

When you've worked through this chapter, you should be better able to:

- list the main purposes which tutor-marked assignments should serve
- use tutor-marked assignments for those purposes
- design assignment questions which prepare your learners as productively as possible for their exams
- compose model answers and feedback comments to give learners maximum benefit
- devise marking schemes in such a way that learners can gain by familiarity with assessment criteria.

Assignments are at the sharp end of open learning. They are the milestones along the open learner's journey. They are an essential ingredient in preparing learners for formal exams, upon which their future careers depend. The first thing to come to mind when thinking about assignments is *assessment* – the score or the grade. But even more important is *feedback* which helps learners with their subject material and allows them to gain from any mistakes they have made in their assignments.

Some tutors will be working at a distance, receiving material mailed by learners; tutor and learner may never meet, although telephone contact is often encouraged. Other tutors – those working on college-based courses – may know their learners; they may have taught them directly.

Tutor-marked assignments involve the learner's work being subjected to human judgement. The tutor will probably give a grade or score. More important, a good tutor will give feedback. Part of this feedback is helping learners over any difficulties shown up by the marked work. Just as important a part is giving praise where it is due and helping to keep learners motivated and interested.

What purposes should assignments serve?

I would suggest that assignments can serve several purposes (which ones are most important will depend on the nature of the course):

- to help learners prepare for formal exams (where relevant)
- to give learners feedback, comment on their work, and develop their self confidence
- to give learners a measure of how successful or otherwise their work is (for example, in relation to exam standards)
- to be a basis for communication between learners and their tutors
- to provide learners with deadlines and stages to help them structure the timing of their work
- to maintain and develop learners' motivation and commitment to their studies.

What are the tools in an assignment toolkit?

- *Questions.* These may be open-ended or structured, depending on the nature of the assignment.
- *Model answers.* These should preferably be composed by the author of the learning material (though they can of course be added by the tutor where not already provided by the author).
- *Marking criteria.* These are devised by the author (or added or adjusted by the tutor).
- *Feedback comments.* Comments on learners' work are written by the tutor. The author can, however, give tutors useful guidelines on this aspect, for example by writing a separate (short) 'tutor guide'.
- *Assessment comments.* Comments relating to performance standards are written by tutors.

Feedback versus scores/grades

Let's first clarify what I mean by these three terms.

Feedback

I'm referring to the *comment* that learners receive about their work. Feedback needs to do a number of things for learners:

- *praise* and reward the learners who got an assignment question right; a mere tick – or a high score – does not do quite enough
- *comfort* learners who got it wrong. 'Red crosses' can turn learners off for life. Learners who've made mistakes need to be reassured that the mistakes were reasonable ones to have made, and that it was in fact useful to have discovered the mistakes
- *direct* learners who got things wrong on how to get them right next time. They need to know how to have another go. They may need an extra question or two to prove to themselves that they can now do it.

Scores/grades

Here I'm referring to any kind of quantitative result. It may be a mark ranging from 0 to 10, or a percentage, or any other number. Or it may be a letter representing a grade.

There are many possible combinations of feedback and scores/grades. Let's think briefly about six of them.

Purely feedback – no mention of scores

This could be tutor feedback or computer-generated feedback (more about this in Chapter 7). The role of such feedback is to praise, comfort and direct – as explained above. Learners are able to tell from such feedback whether they have done brilliantly or otherwise. It may be kinder to learners who have done poorly not to have a score to show just *how* poorly they have done.

Feedback with scores that are not important

Feedback (as described above) can be accompanied by a quantitative measure of performance, with reassuring words like 'Don't take too much notice of your score – these are "fun" scores at this stage, that don't count in your final grading.

Feedback with scores that count

This is self-explanatory. The scores will, of course, be taken more seriously by learners.

Feedback with detailed scoring breakdown

Obviously, such scoring counts towards assessment. However, the detail in itself may be very useful to learners, allowing them to see exactly where they have gained or lost marks.

Assessment record only

This may be a printout of a learner's record of achievement. It may help the learner to see the general pattern of his or her progress over a number of assignments or tasks. It can also help tutors to identify the strengths and weaknesses of learners – and to give help accordingly.

Assessment (or score) only

The most obvious example is the exam result. Learners are informed of their scores, but don't get much (or any) feedback regarding what was correct and what wasn't.

What do learners look for first?

The score or grade! All learners getting back an assignment want to know straight away how well (or badly) they have done. If the score is at the end of several pages, learners will thumb through quickly until they find it. I'd go as far as to suggest that the score can completely eclipse the feedback!

Let's imagine three learners, Janet (a high-flier), John (an average learner) and Jim (he's struggling).

Janet's score is 85 per cent (or grade A). What does she do? She's quite likely to say to herself 'Great!' But is she likely to look carefully at the feedback? Will she check to see exactly where she lost the missing 15 per cent of her score? I think not. And who can blame her? She's done well. But the feedback may well have proved useful to her – even if she didn't need it very much.

John's score is 60 per cent (or grade C). He's passed, he's all right. Will he bother to look at the feedback in detail? He may well be relieved to have passed another assignment and be most concerned now to press on and try to pass the next one.

Jim failed! His score was 35 per cent (or grade E). What does he do? Does he carefully look through the marked work for all the comments that explain exactly what went wrong, and what to do next time? Or does he take one look at that score and tear up the assignment in disgust? I've watched that happen. However useful the feedback could have been, it was lost for ever.

What can we do about scores and feedback?

I've been trying to show that when learners get scores and feedback at the same instant, the scores may dominate at the expense of the feedback.

If it is necessary for score and feedback to reach learners at the same time, I think the best way is to make it possible for them to check exactly how the score was arrived at, for example by referring to a model answer and marking scheme.

But it might be better if the marked assignment reached learners with feedback comments only. Learners would go searching diligently through all the comments, trying to tell whether they had done well or not. So at least the feedback would be being used. The tutor could give the score a week or so later in a telephone discussion (or in a subsequent face-to-face session if such existed). The learners would have had the opportunity to benefit from the feedback without being distracted by the score.

I hope I've convinced you that learners (especially open learners) will take any score or grade you give them very seriously. They're likely to feel that you're assessing *them*, not just their work. On the one hand, you may be obliged to make their scores realistic to prepare them for the standard of some forthcoming exam. On the other hand, you need to try to prevent them being blinded to the feedback you give them. It's a dilemma sometimes. An important part of the solution is to make the scoring as 'open' as possible. Let your learners see exactly how their scores are arrived at. Let them learn from your scoring criteria, as well as from the feedback comments you provide.

Let learners guess their scores or grades

If you know your learners relatively well (for example if you're working with them on programmes involving some face-to-face contact, or if you've been communicating at a distance for some time), it can be worth inviting learners to guess their scores or grades, and write them on their own work when they send it to you for marking. You may be surprised by how many of their guesses are accurate. This process gives you the chance to diagnose those learners who are far too modest about their work (not a dangerous problem), and also those who have not yet realized that their work is still falling some considerable way behind their own expectations of it (a much more dangerous problem).

Let's now go on to think in some detail about the optimum design of the most common sort of assignment – the tutor-marked assignment.

Design of TMAs

I suggest below a checklist of criteria for the design of useful tutor-marked assignment questions. (It's rarely possible to fulfil all these criteria in one's initial design, and ways of improving assignments during and after the piloting stage are discussed subsequently.)

Is the question clear and unambiguous?

Will each learner interpret it in the way it was intended to be read? More marks are lost in exams through misinterpretation of questions than from ignorance.

Does the question directly relate to stated learning objectives?

How unfair it is for learners to be asked to do something that didn't seem to be on the agenda.

Have learners been adequately prepared for the question (for example through self-assessment questions)?

I'm not suggesting that learners should already have done exactly the same questions, but that the self-assessment questions or other material should have helped them develop the skills and knowledge that they need to answer the tutor-marked assignment questions.

Are there several ways of answering the question properly?

This may be fine, but it does mean that alternative marking schemes may be needed for the variety of answers. It's usually easier in the long run to make the question so that there is only really one best way of tackling it.

Does it prepare learners for the sort of question that may be met in formal assessments or exams?

Of course, the tutor-marked assignment may itself be a formal assessment! But if an exam is coming up later, the tutor feedback on exam-like questions can be most useful to learners.

For the learner, is the main purpose of the question assessment or feedback?

If the main purpose is assessment, the marking scheme needs to be very watertight and polished. If the main purpose is feedback, the marks may well not count, and the tutor response can be orientated towards helping learners.

If the assignment is to be used for assessment, can learners tell how many marks go with each question?

Learners are very good at matching effort to marks. If one thing carries ten marks and another carries only two, they know where to spend most of their time. It is useful to show learners:

   how many marks go with each question – especially when some are worth more than others
   how many marks go with the different parts of any longer questions.

Will it be useful to prepare a model answer (or answers) to issue to learners along with feedback?

Model answers can make it quicker to give direct, appropriate feedback to each learner. Of course, it may happen that model answers get circulated between learners who know each other, but that doesn't happen as often as you might think.

Does the assignment as a whole test the main things the learner needs?

It's all too easy for an assignment to test a particular part of what the learner needs to know because that part happens to be easier to test.

Does the assignment begin with fairly easy questions?

The most difficult stage in doing a TMA is very often getting started. Learners can be eased into the assignment by a few questions which are less demanding than those to come.

Have 'either/or' choices been built-in where appropriate (such as for learners with different needs or interests)?

Learning materials can be designed to serve a variety of learners with different needs, abilities and experience. The same tutor can give appropriate feedback to each sort of learner. Of course, this 'differentiation' is not possible if all the learners are aiming at the same examination standard.

TMAs are serious stuff

The average open learner takes tutor-marked assignments – particularly the very first one – very seriously.

When learners send in a tutor-marked assignment, they are submitting themselves to the judgment of someone they perceive as an expert. It may be the first time for years that they have done this. Imagine how you would feel as an open learner sending in your very first tutor-marked assignment. You don't yet know your tutor and you've not been assessed by a tutor or anybody else for years, perhaps since schooldays! You'd probably be experiencing a mixture of strong emotions and have lots of questions buzzing around in your head. Here are some of the things learners have told me they felt at the point of sending in their first tutor-marked assignment:

- apprehensive (most say this!)
- vulnerable
- exposed
- excited
- will he think I'm an idiot?
- it is good enough?
- when will I know how I've done?
- I hope she can read it!
- have I made a fool of myself?
- did I do enough?
- will he be gentle with me?

- why did I start this course?
- I'm glad that's over!
- when can I get on with section 2?
- oh, blow it, I did my best!

Assignments are often a very emotional, possibly painful, part of the open learning experience. So there's no place where we have to be more careful in our use of words, making sure we communicate clearly and unambiguously.

Some examples for discussion

TUTOR-MARKED ASSIGNMENT I

Write a short open learning sample package, of between ten and 15 pages. You can write this in your own subject area, or in any subject area of your choice.

Assessment scheme:

clear objectives	5
three or more self-assessment questions	15
real *responses* to each self-assessment question (not just answers to the questions)	15
informal, friendly style	2
clear, short sentences	2
stimulating introduction	3
helpful review or summary	2
good links between the objectives and self-assessment questions	2
good use of headings and subheadings	2
feedback questionnaire	2
	50

Comments

This tutor-marked assignment could be used as part of a training programme for open learning writers. Note how the 'assessment scheme' shows the writers exactly what to include in their specimen open learning package, and also makes a number of points about the relative importance of the components (for example, many marks are associated with the design of self-assessment questions and responses, to emphasize that designing these is one of the most important steps in the process of putting together open learning material). Learners (in this case writers) could self-assess their work against each of the headings in the assessment scheme, or could peer-assess each other's work. Of course, the tutor could do the assessing for them too.

TUTOR-MARKED ASSIGNMENT 2

Explore the advantages and disadvantages of the following teaching–learning situations:

- large-group lectures
- small-group tutorials
- student-led seminars
- directed private study
- student team projects
- computer conferencing

In each case:

- list five advantages of the method   5
- list five disadvantages of the method   5
- explain how you would use it in your own work   5

Add a set of recommendations for choosing which strategy
to use for which purposes   10
                                                                        100

Comments

This is in many respects a very broad assignment, suitable for use in training-the trainers courses or staff-development programmes in colleges. If the question had *not* included the 'in each case' details, it would have been very difficult for learners to work out exactly how to approach the assignment, or indeed to what approximate depth their answers might be expected to go. However, when briefed to find five advantages and disadvantages of each method, their task becomes much more specific – and it can be seen that one 'mark' goes with each of them.

There are many possibilities for adding further structure to this assignment. However, if it becomes too structured, learners' scope for creativity and lateral thinking are reduced. Some of the extra 'riders' which could be incorporated in the assessment breakdown could include:

- references to relevant discussions in the literature   20
- linking each process to the ways in which learners learn   20
- comments on relative cost-effectiveness of each method   10

TUTOR-MARKED ASSIGNMENT 3

Write a proposal (1500–2000 words) for a new reservoir.

Assessment scheme:

- rationale for building and siting the reservoir   10
- geological summary of the area involved   8
- sketch map, showing before/after flooding   8
- discussion of environmental factors   8
- flowchart showing construction processes and timescales   8
- details of dam design   8

                                                             50

Comments

This is similar to a real assignment that I mark on an open learning course which introduces the principles of technology to learners intending to continue with an Open University Foundation Course. The task proposed by the question itself is impossibly vague: 'Write a proposal (1500–2000 words) for a new reservoir.' However, with just a few lines of further detail (including the marks allocation) the task becomes quite manageable.

It is often useful to include word limits in tutor-marked assignment questions (and it is common practice in Open University assignments). However, I prefer to give a 'bandwidth' rather than a definitive limit. If one says 'about 2000 words', some learners will take it very literally, and count their words exactly, artificially adjusting their work to get a particular total word count, and put in brackets at the end '2003 words'! Others will more or less ignore the suggestion altogether, and happily send in 4000 words. Giving a range (such as 1500–2000 words) helps avoid either extreme.

When you've got a pile of assignments to mark, and when the marks 'count', it's obviously important to be as fair and objective as possible. This is easier when:

- all the learners have done the task on approximately the same scale
- their answers are all structured within a similar framework.

Designing a marking scheme

As you may have gathered from the examples we have just explored, designing a 'solid' marking scheme is well worth the effort. Where a single tutor is marking all the assignments, it is tempting not to bother with marking schemes at all. However, the quality of assessment is increasingly under scrutiny in education and training. Armed with detailed marking schemes, you have evidence to show anyone who needs to be convinced that your assessing procedures are not ad-hoc but well thought out.

In the past, marking was often done subjectively. When it came to deciding scores or grades for assignments (and exam answers), there was quite a lot of 'put down the number you first thought of' going on. This may have been quicker than rigorous, objective assessment, but it certainly was not fairer. Now, with learning outcomes and performance criteria much more 'on the table' for all to see, there is no excuse for sloppy assessment. In the long run, in fact, assessment is made both quicker and easier when it's done thoroughly, systematically and objectively.

If you write an open learning module which becomes popular or published, your assignments will have to be marked by lots of other tutors. For other people to mark your assignments well, it's essential to have a marking scheme to indicate clearly how many marks are scored by each component or step. A good marking scheme will usually deal carefully with 'borderline' issues – what gets each available mark, and what loses it.

A good marking scheme can also be a valuable instrument to share with learners, who can gain much valuable information about where credit is gained (or lost). Giving learners the chance to see and apply assessment criteria is one of the most effective ways of letting them gather feedback about their work. I stressed in Chapters 1 and 2 how important feedback is as an intrinsic part of the way that people learn. The assessment schemes that I included in my discussion examples of tutor-marked assignments were quite simple yet they would give learners a great deal of help in structuring their answers. The assessment details also help to remind learners that large assignments can be broken down into a number of manageable tasks, and these can be tackled one step at a time.

The 'culture' of assessment varies considerably from one discipline to another. The assignment themes I addressed in my discussion examples were relatively 'soft', with a great deal of room for manoeuvre for learners. In maths, science and engineering, assessment schemes can be much 'harder'. In other words, where answers are either right or wrong, the allocation of marks can be made much more 'black and white' than in the examples I gave (and it is considerably easier to design marking schemes). Next, I will present a checklist to use in devising marking schemes.

Designing marking schemes: a checklist

Could *anyone* mark any assignment and agree its score within a mark of two?

This may seem a formidable criterion – it is! But in many national exams, teams of examiners have to be able to mark scripts to an accuracy of about 1 per cent.

Does the scheme allow credit for alternative good answers?

If the tutor-marked assignment question is at all ambiguous, the scheme may need to cater for learners interpreting the question in different but equally correct ways. The marking scheme needs to allow for all reasonable alternatives, fairly.

Does the scheme distribute marks fairly, according to the relative importance of different components of answers?

Ideally, the questions themselves will have made it clear to learners where the marks lie. The marking scheme needs on the one hand to be faithful to the question; while on the other hand giving fair credit for everything learners have got correct.

Does the scheme allow 'consequential' marks when an early mistake affects later parts of an answer?

This particularly applies to calculation-type questions. If a mistake is made early in an answer but all subsequent steps are done correctly, a good marking scheme will give credit for each correct step *operation*, despite the fact that the final answer was wrong. So, a learner could end up with 18 out of 20 marks, even for a 'wrong' final answer.

Could the marking scheme be issued to learners, for them to mark their own assignments?

This is a useful practice for early assignments, or dry-run preparation for exams, when learners may benefit from being able to discover their mistakes in private.

Is the standard of marking as close as possible to that of any formal tests or exams the learners may be preparing for?

It would be very sad if an open learner consistently got 80 per cent in tutor-marked assignments then failed a national exam. It's well worth using every trick in the trade to find out what the *real* marking criteria are going to be. That may mean signing up as an examiner yourself!

Does the marking scheme remove 'subjective' marking?

Scratching one's head then putting down a number between one and 20 – perhaps the number one first thought of. It's terrible to treat learners' work so callously, but it happens. Even from the tutor's point of view, surely it's more comfortable to know that the marking is objective and fair; to know that if you have a bad day tomorrow, your marking will still be as fair as it is today.

Could the marking scheme be issued to learners, along with a model answer, to show them exactly how the assignment should best be tackled?

I've proved to my own satisfaction that my students have learned more from my marking schemes than from my lectures or handouts! The thing about a marking scheme is that students identify themselves closely with its use – they concentrate. They see from it what gains credit. And they see from it what *loses* marks: they never make those mistakes again!

Does the scheme make it quicker and easier to mark assignments?

I've often had on my desk a pile of 400 exam scripts. I've learned over the years that the first 50 will take about a third of the total time, and about half of the total sweat! Once the marking scheme is thoroughly learned and understood, each decision of 'to award or not to award' becomes much easier to make; marking speeds up greatly. Therefore, for anyone expecting to mark a fair number of assignments, even if over a long period of time, a good marking scheme soon pays for itself in terms of time saved.

Could the marking scheme, along with model answers, be published in a future edition of the study material as an exemplar?

This is the real challenge. How many of us are prepared to put our assessment criteria up for public scrutiny? However, think of the boost to the credibility of open learning materials which do just this. Open learning is learner-centred, and this entails letting learners in on everything.

A demanding list of criteria, I think you'll agree. But a marking scheme is written once, then used many times. Of course, it will be modified according to experience gained while using it, and it will get better and better. A marking scheme must not be an afterthought, something done in a rush at the last minute. The best time to design the marking scheme is at the time the questions themselves (and model answers) are being designed, with the details of the learning outcomes – particularly performance criteria – firmly in sight.

Improving assignments during piloting

If you write a complete open learning package, the assignments are the thing you'll want to change first. Your open learning text may need minimal adjustments during piloting. Your self-assessment questions and responses may only need the odd bit of clarification here and there. But tutor-marked assignments are another matter! However good assignment questions are, they won't be perfect at first.

In practice, it's well worth considering having the tutor-marked assignments in a separate booklet (or even on loose sheets) rather than including them in the body of an open learning module. It's then much easier to revise and amend the assignments without needing to change the open learning material itself.

Changes to help learners

You may want to make changes and adjustments to tutor-marked assignments after the whole package has been printed. For this reason it is a good idea to have the assignments printed separately. The text in the module need simply say 'Now please complete assignment no. 1 supplied separately and return it to your tutor.'

After the first 50 learners have worked through the assignments, you'll know where changes are needed in the questions:

- changes to stop learners running off at tangents
- changes to prevent learners from misinterpreting questions – even questions you thought were impossible to misinterpret
- changes of emphasis, to help learners identify what the real points of some of the questions are; the odd underlining of a key word may make all the difference
- changes in length of assignment: feedback from learners often shows that what were intended to be 'equal' assignments turn out to be far from equal in practice.

Even *before* the open learning material is produced (or written), try out the assignment questions on a small pilot group of learners. If possible use some 'live' students – you can ask them things as well as analyse their work. Take notice of things most of them do well, and of common mistakes. The mistakes may well be your fault.

Changes to help tutors

It's a good idea to get a few different tutors to mark the first batches of assignments during piloting of open learning material. Better still, have some pilot learner assignments photocopied and marked by *each* of several tutors separately. If the marks agree more or less you may be justly proud of your hard work on the marking scheme.

In the light of the pilot experience, you'll want to make changes to the questions themselves:

- when learners find them too hard
- when learners find them too easy
- when misinterpretation often happens
- when tutors find them hard to mark fairly
- when there turn out to be several ways of answering the question well.

You'll also want to make changes to the marking schemes:

- when allocating marks fairly proves difficult
- when agreement on the 'score' of a specimen assignment is hard to reach among several tutors
- when important parts of the answer need to carry more credit, so that learners see what's important.

Changes to enhance credibility

Here I'm thinking of changes which might be required, perhaps at a later stage, when looking at the learning material as a whole:

- fine-tuning questions and marking to those standards that the learners will face from external examining bodies and so on
- spreading credit more fairly over the course as a whole
- changes to reflect new perspectives or emphases as the subject itself develops.

Conclusions

I hope the above will have impressed you with the importance of putting all of your skills and experience into the design of tutor-marked assignment questions and marking schemes.

Tutor-marked assignments, more than anything else, reflect exactly what learners are becoming able to do. A good set of learners' answers is the best evidence you can accumulate for the quality of their learning – and of your programme.

Assignments are the 'sharp end' of open learning materials, not least in the eyes of the learners. Assignments are the way in which learners can prove themselves to themselves as well as to outsiders such as tutors. It matters a lot that they are given every chance to do themselves full justice.

Chapter 7

Computer-marked Assignments

Abstract

Computer-marked assignments are increasingly being used to support open and flexible learning. Such assignments lend themselves best to the kind of structured questions suitable for self-assessment questions – in other words, where it is possible to package-up feedback in a form where it applies to the ways most learners tackle particular sets of questions. The principles used in composing computer-marked assignments also extend to designing computer-based interactive flexible learning programmes. In such programmes, the feedback given on-screen when learners make choices or enter information via the keyboard is of the sort which may have been given by a 'live' tutor.

Objectives

By the end of this chapter, you should be able to:

■ extend the principles of writing self-assessment questions and responses outlined in Chapter 4 (particularly multiple-choice format) to computer-marked assignments (CMAs) and feedback response elements
■ include in the computer feedback suitable introductory and concluding paragraphs
■ decide the optimum balance between feedback and assessment in your computer-marked assignments (in light of the discussion in Chapter 6)
■ use computer-marked assignment formats to gather information about learners' experiences of various aspects of their studies.

I'm assuming that you've looked in detail at certain earlier parts of this book. Before reading on, you may wish quickly to look back at a few topics which are important here:

■ Chapter 4: self-assessment question and response design, particularly multiple-choice questions

- Chapter 5: readability and 'action language' are directly relevant to the design of such feedback
- Chapter 6: I went to some lengths trying to help you to think about open learners' feelings about being assessed by a tutor. Similar feelings are bound to exist regarding computer-based assessment. I'd like you particularly to continue to bear in mind the 'feedback versus scores/grades' discussion.

What is a computer-marked assignment?

A computer-marked assignment in open learning schemes is one where learners' answers are processed by a computer. For this to happen, learners' answers need to be relatively simple to process. The most common choice for such assignments is multiple-choice questions. These usually involve four options – learners choose the one they think most likely to be correct. Learners then fill in the letters corresponding to the chosen options on forms or cards. At the marking location, the learners' responses will be keyed into the computer (or 'optically read'), and the computer will then process the choices in terms of which are correct and which aren't.

The story could end there, with the learner simply being sent a score. However, the computer can do much more than this – and very quickly. The computer can print out a *feedback* response to each of the learners' choices. In this way, the computer can 'reply' to each learner individually, depending on which questions were answered correctly or wrongly.

Of course, the computer doesn't design the responses! Human skills and experience are needed for that. The writer of each question is the best person to decide exactly what will be said to learners. Especially important is deciding exactly what message should reach the learner who picks a wrong option.

With interactive learning programmes increasingly being computer-based, 'computer-marked assignment' now has an alternative meaning: an assignment which learners do, sitting at a computer or terminal, where their decisions and answers to questions are instantly 'marked', recorded and processed by a computer, and where feedback can be instantly given to learners.

In Chapter 4 we explored quite fully the things to bear in mind when responding to learners' choices. Just a reminder about one key point: learners need a response to what *they* did – the option they chose. If it was wrong, they need to know why they made the mistake. So a typical response to a wrong choice of option would look something like this:

Question 5
You chose option (c). Sorry, but it wouldn't do to have a digital voltmeter with an input impedance of 10 ohms. Such a low impedance would effectively short out the circuit whose voltages you wished to measure. The best meters have input impedances of over 1000000 ohms (1 Megaohm). When you chose '10 ohms' you were probably thinking of the conditions needed to measure *resistance* not voltage. Most of us confuse the two at first.

What bits make up a computer-marked assignment?

We've mentioned the most important components of computer-marked assignments – questions and responses. A typical computer-marked assignment may involve ten four-option multiple-choice questions. That means, of course, that 40 responses need to be written. Since any learner will only see one response to each question, each of the responses needs to be self-sufficient. Writing the responses to a set of computer-marked assignment questions takes most of the time, and much of the care.

However, a good reply to a computer-marked assignment is more than just a set of responses. It should be more like a personal letter to the learner. At least, it needs:

- an introductory bit
- a concluding bit.

The introductory bit can be the start of a letter. The computer is easily programmed to start a reply with 'Dear ...', filling in the learner's first name. Friendly remarks such as 'Thanks for sending in computer-marked assignment 5' can be slotted in. General comments can be included, such as 'Most people find that question 8 is the tricky one in this computer-marked assignment.' If you're designing several consecutive computer-marked assignments, try to make their introductory bits different. The more 'human' the computer-generated letter appears to be, the better it serves your learners. An introductory bit could look something like this:

> Dear Jack,
> Thanks for sending in computer-marked assignment 5. Some of the questions in this assignment were harder than they looked! Below, I've replied regarding the options you chose for each of the ten questions in turn. It would be useful to you to look again at the assignment questions to remind yourself of the choices you made.

The concluding bit can serve a variety of purposes. It can advise about the next assignment. It can give a general comment about the performance. For example, suppose there were ten questions in the computer-marked assignment. There could be different concluding bits depending on score. A highly complimentary one could go to learners who got all questions right. A milder form of praise could go to learners who got eight or nine questions right. A strong message of encouragement may be needed by learners who got two or fewer right!

An example of a concluding paragraph is given below:

> As you saw above, you got seven out of the ten questions right – that's good. All were right except the ones testing section 5.8 of the module. It's worth you having another look at this section I think. Otherwise, everything's splendid.

The next computer-marked assignment has ten questions on unit 6. It's worth giving special attention to section 6.3 – that's where most people have problems! Good luck – I look forward to computer-marked assignment 6.

Scores

We looked at this issue in some detail in Chapter 6; the same considerations still apply. It's very easy indeed to instruct the computer to award a score. For example, the correct option to each question could score ten marks. A ten-question test would total 100, and the final score would conveniently look like a percentage. Alternatively, some questions may be more important or difficult than others, and could be given scores to reflect this. Learners would need to know this as they made their choices. But what about the incorrect options? It would be simple if they were all quite wrong, and scored zero marks each. But are they equally wrong? Or is there a next best option, and might this be worth eight marks, or six marks – or what? This is the problem with scoring multiple-choice questions. Some options are better than others, and it's very hard to decide how much the less-than-perfect options should earn. If you want to score them, the best way of deciding how many marks to award to each incorrect option is to take the average of several people's opinions. The final score can be built into either the introductory or concluding paragraphs of the computer-printed feedback. For example:

Dear Sian,
Thanks for sending in assignment 3. Congratulations, you've scored 85 per cent. Please look below to remind yourself of all the things you did correctly, and to find one or two areas where you may like to refresh your memory.

or

Dear David,
... Now that you've explored the responses to your choices of options, it's time for your score – 55 per cent. That's just about a pass, but the important thing is you now know exactly which points you need to explore further.

It's still worth bearing in mind how the score can distract from the feedback. That said, people do like to be given scores – especially good ones!

Other uses of computer-marked assignments

Gaining feedback about the learning materials

Think about the following sorts of question in computer-marked assignment form. (There wouldn't be a score to the questions below, of course.)

11   Which of the following did you personally find most helpful?
   A   the self-assessment questions and responses
   B   the objectives
   C   the text itself
   D   the review
12   Which section do you think was the most successful in Module 3?
   A   section 1 on causes of corrosion
   B   section 2 on prevention of corrosion
   C   section 3 on theory of corrosion
   D   section 4 on pourbaix diagrams
13   In general, what is your opinion of the style of the materials?
   A   easy to follow
   B   fairly easy to follow
   C   rather difficult to follow
   D   very difficult to follow
14   How interesting did you find Module 3 in general?
   A   very interesting
   B   mostly interesting
   C   sometimes interesting
   D   rarely interesting
15   Approximately how long did it take you to study Module 4?
   A   more than ten hours
   B   between six and ten hours
   C   between three and six hours
   D   less than three hours

Such questions have the advantage that learners simply tick boxes or fill in letters on a simple form – quicker, easier and more anonymous than having to express opinions longhand. There are all sorts of similar questions which could be used to obtain feedback about chosen aspects of the learning materials. The computer could be programmed to build up files giving statistical analysis of the responses to each of the questions. This can make it much easier to assess learners' views objectively.

Although there may be no need for responses to such questions, it is possible to give useful comments as part of the computer-generated feedback. For example, let's take one of the questions above:

11   Which of the following did you personally find most helpful?
   A   the self-assessment questions and responses
   B   the objectives
   C   the text itself
   D   the review

Each of the learners receives a response according to the options they chose. The purpose here is simply to give the impression that their views are being taken into account, and that it was worthwhile choosing options. Of course, each learner sees only one of these responses:

11A   We're glad you found the self-assessment questions and responses useful. They are opportunities for you to practise things, and to find out for yourself how you're getting on with your studies.

11B   Good. You found the objectives helpful. They are indeed intended to help you find out exactly what you need to be able to do to succeed in your studies.

11C   We're glad you found the text useful. It may be worth trying to make more use of the self-assessment questions and responses, which are there to make sure you're getting enough practice at the things the text deals with.

11D   We're glad you found the review useful to you personally. Reviews can indeed be a quick way of reminding yourself about the main ideas in your learning materials. Don't forget, however, to give yourself plenty of practice at *doing* things – that's what the self-assessment questions and responses are there for.

Gathering information about tutor support

The advantage of the computer-marked assignment format is that learners are more willing to tick boxes or pick options than to express views about tutor support directly.

For example, the following questions could be asked:

16   How useful are you finding the feedback you receive on your tutor-marked assignments from your tutor?
    A   very useful
    B   quite useful
    C   not very useful
    D   not at all useful

17   How do you feel about the time it takes to get tutor-marked assignments back from your tutor?
    A   feedback comes quickly
    B   I'd like feedback more quickly
    C   the delay is much too long
    D   the delay doesn't really matter

18   How do you feel about your tutor?
    A   my tutor is very helpful and encouraging
    B   my tutor is quite helpful and encouraging
    C   my tutor is not really helpful and encouraging
    D   my tutor is quite unhelpful and discouraging!

19   How do you feel about the grades or scores your tutor gives?
      A   very fair
      B   fair enough
      C   I don't feel they're fair
      D   my tutor doesn't give grades or scores

While the purpose of such questions may be simply to gather information, it is still possible to reply to learners' choices with appropriate comments in computer-marked-assignment response style, so that learners are aware that their views have been noted.

   Where several tutors are working in parallel, the sort of data collected through such questions can be useful in diagnosing tutors' strengths and weaknesses. Of course, it would be advisable to follow up any negative comments in more detail before drawing any firm conclusions – a learner may just be prejudiced or unrealistic.

Helping learners

Of course, *everything* should be designed to help learners, but I'm thinking here of support with study-skills development. For example, suppose the following question was included:

20   What are your present feelings about your forthcoming exam?
      A   I'm scared stiff!
      B   I'm rather apprehensive
      C   I'm becoming more confident
      D   I'm already confident

Responses could give appropriate messages of sympathy or encouragement to learners selecting each of the options. For example, a learner choosing option B could be counselled as follows:

20B   So you're rather apprehensive about your forthcoming exam? This is perfectly natural – and healthy! When we're a little bit nervous, it helps us focus our minds and ensure that sufficient preparation gets done. You'll find that the more you put into preparing for the exam, the less nervous you get about it. When you begin to feel that you can tackle just about any question that could be asked, you may even feel pleasantly confident and brave. One of the best ways to develop your confidence is to practise answering exam questions. The more you practise, the easier it gets. More important perhaps, the quicker you get at writing down your answers. So, don't leave your revision to the day before the exam – do some *now* and you'll soon feel less apprehensive.

The following message may suit someone who selected option D:

20D You're already confident about your forthcoming exam? Good – it's a
     pleasant feeling. However, don't let your confidence get in the way of
     checking out that you're well practised at doing what you need to in the
     exam – write answers to exam questions. Remember, it's what you *write*
     that counts at the end of the day (not just what you know). So put in a bit
     of practice at writing answers to typical exam questions, just to give you
     a solid basis for that confident feeling.

Conclusions

As we noted in Chapter 4, multiple-choice questions have a somewhat tarnished
reputation in educational circles, but they can serve many purposes as computer-
marked assignments. As *feedback* questions they are very useful. As well as being
usable in distance learning schemes, all types of computer-generated feedback
can be designed into 'live' computer-based learning packages, where the same
principles of giving feedback to learners have the additional advantage that the
feedback can be given instantly. Let's end by briefly reviewing some of the
advantages of multiple-choice questions as the basis of computer-marked
assignments.

- The computer can respond very quickly to individual learners making
  different errors.
- The computer doesn't get tired! The computer will patiently 'explain' the
  cause of a common mistake to as many learners as there are. Humans tend to
  get bored doing this – and take short cuts.
- The computer doesn't get fed up of saying 'That's absolutely right' or 'Don't
  worry, most of us have mixed this up at one time or another' or 'Question 5
  was the hardest question in the set' and so on.
- The computer can churn out a detailed set of feedback responses in a much
  shorter time than a human tutor. This means feedback gets to the learner
  much faster – before the questions have been forgotten! It's reckoned that
  the usefulness of feedback fades rapidly if it takes a long time to come. With
  self-assessment questions the response can be immediate. With computer-
  marked assignments the response is still considerably faster than the average
  tutor-marked-assignment feedback response.
- Multiple-choice questions can be used to gather information about how
  learners feel about many aspects of their studies. On some issues, learners
  may find it easier to pick options than to express their views openly.
  Responses to such questions can reassure learners that their views are being
  noted.

Chapter 8

Tutoring Open Learners

Abstract

I'm assuming in this chapter that you've already looked at Chapter 6 on designing tutor-marked assignments. I'm also hoping that this has convinced you of:

- the importance of feedback, rather than just scores or grades
- the importance of objectivity in marking work
- the importance of making good use of model answers and assessment criteria.

In this chapter I'm using the term 'tutoring' to cover a number of things. These include:

- *assessment:* marking assignment work and providing advice and guidance where mistakes have been made
- *tutoring:* providing tuition either face-to-face or at a distance through written or telephone communication
- *counselling:* giving more general support and guidance, including helping open learners develop and maintain their motivation, and assisting them develop their learning skills.

In this chapter, I'd like us to explore the 'human' communication side of tutoring. This chapter is addressed directly to open learning tutors and other people such as 'mentors' who may help open learners. If you are *in charge* of tutors or mentors (rather than actually teaching) perhaps you can pass on the ideas I'm putting to you.

Objectives

By the end of this chapter, I trust that you'll be ready to be:

an effective open learning tutor
someone who makes a lot of positive difference to your learners' experiences of open learning.

Do Open Learners need tutoring?

If open learning materials were perfect, and if learners' learning skills were highly developed, there might be no need for tutoring. Even with imperfect learning materials, many learners soldier on and succeed without the help of a tutor. Many open learners have no choice – there just isn't a tutor anyway.

But most open learners would like some support. Even with the best of open learning materials, a good tutor can make all the difference to the learners voyage. At the same time, it must be admitted that a poor tutor can do untold harm to learners' self-esteem and motivation. The essence of good tutoring lies in being responsive to learners' needs. A good starting point is to think about the learners themselves.

Who are open learners?

You may think that this question should have been asked much earlier in this book! When designing open learning materials, the better your picture of the sorts of people who may use them, the easier it is for you to write for them. However, in some respects, it's the open learning *tutors* who have the closest relationship to open learners, so I've left this discussion till now.

There may well be all sorts of different people studying your learning materials, but we must never forget that they're all individuals, each with their own hopes, fears, needs and ambitions. Having said that, there may be a few common characteristics:

Keen to get started away

Open learners tend to be high on motivation. They've usually made a definite decision – to start. Of course, at any time they can decide to stop. As a tutor you've got to try and prevent them from stopping. Above all, you've got to make sure that anything you write to them or say to them doesn't turn out to be the last straw that breaks the camel's back!

Good reasons for choosing to learn, and for choosing open learning in particular

Many open learners have chosen *not* to go for a more formal course of education or training. They won't want to be treated like schoolchildren but as experienced, responsible adults – they probably *are* experienced, responsible adults!

Feeling vulnerable and exposed

Many people who choose an open learning system have bad memories of conventional education. They may have experienced failure or have felt unable to make progress. Whatever subsequent experience they have gained, they may still be afraid when they return to studying.

Needing help to work on their own

For much of the time, they'll be working by themselves. They need to feel involved in their learning materials. You can do a lot to help this process, as discussed in Chapter 5, by using informal, friendly language.

Having limited time to study

The open learning programme isn't going to be the only thing in their lives! They may have full-time jobs. Many of your learners may have demanding families. They may have very limited time for studying. You can help them by breaking down their studies into manageable chunks. There are many more free ten-minute spells in a busy person's week than there are free two-hour spells.

Needing help in using textbooks

Some of their learning may have to come from textbooks rather than from purpose-built open learning packages. Many textbooks are relatively indigestible, and it can make all the difference if you can help them know exactly what they're supposed to be getting out of their textbook episodes. A few words of advice from you may turn what might have been an hour's passive reading into an hour's productive learning.

Needing convincing that open learning really works

For many open learners, the processes and responsibilities are quite new, and they may not yet believe in their own ability to handle them.

Wondering where they'll find the time

This applies equally to open learners working on their own at a distance as to students or trainees doing conventional courses with the addition of some open learning components. Time-management skills are essential for all kinds of open-learners – and it's usually open learning tutors that are first to find out when learners lack these.

Making your own learner profiles

Still thinking of your learners as individuals, it's useful to build up profiles of the type of people who may be involved in your own open learning scene. You can do this by answering questions like these for two or three 'typical' sorts of learner:

- who are they? (It's even useful to make up names for them if you haven't any real ones yet)
- what are their *reasons* for learning?
- why have they chosen *open* learning?
- what sort of past experience have they?
- what could be their main problems with open learning?
- where will they do most of their learning?
- what could be their main strengths?
- how much time have they for studying?
- have they any fears or anxieties about studying or assessment?
- how will open learning relate to the rest of their lives?
- will they have access to peer-group support?
- what will they *expect* from an open learning tutor?
- what will they *need* from a tutor?

The questions above can be the basis for some very useful 'case studies' of the characteristics of people who may become open learners. Moreover, many of the same issues can be addressed in 'getting to know you' activities conducted by open learning tutors with new learners. It's possible to design a simple questionnaire for learners to complete based on questions such as those above. Alternatively, the questions can form the basis of an 'interview checklist', where learners and tutors have the chance of face-to-face introductions.

Let's now go on to explore how learners *feel*. Of course, their feelings will change as their studies progress, and tutors will have to adjust accordingly. A good tutor will need a range of different skills to help learners through the different stages of their voyage.

Let's start at the beginning. This is the time when learners may decide that they're not equipped for the voyage. They may be quite wrong to decide this - and even when they're right, the good tutor can often find for them a voyage more suitable to their resources.

How do open learners feel at the beginning?

Suppose it's the very first time that a person has tackled open learning. The learning package may look daunting as well as stimulating. What sort of feeling has the learner got at the start of the programme? We can assume that they will be a mixture of the following:

Excited

They may be expecting a lot. They may be very eager to get started - so eager, in fact, that there's the danger of skimming through any explanations regarding the best way of working through the package, preferring to dive in at the start of the subject material itself.

Apprehensive

It may be the first time any learning has been attempted for some time (many years sometimes). Some learners feel a bit afraid of what they may have let themselves in for.

Curious

Many will not have been *open* learners before. Such learners will need reassurance that it is indeed possible for them to learn under their own steam. They will need help in building confidence to organize their studies constructively.

Exposed and vulnerable

The learning may carry with it some form of assessment; it may have been a long time since the learner had his or her work marked or graded. Some learners may have failed the last exam or assessment they took – perhaps many years ago. Many fear the 'judgements' to come!

Inadequate

Many learners have doubts about their ability to succeed. The learning materials may look quite daunting, especially to those learners who skim ahead and see all sorts of things coming up that they have not heard of before. They may well be wondering 'Have I got to learn every word, diagram, chart and table in the material?' Of course they haven't got to learn the whole package – just achieve its objectives and answer questions up to a prescribed standard. But how can they tell this?

The above picture is obviously a generalization. It would be more useful to *ask* your learners how they feel, by phone or in writing. Giving learners the chance to open up to you can make a lot of difference in breaking down any barriers.

Learners' needs in mid-course

Learners often get 'mid-course blues'. Some of the novelty may have worn off, the subject matter is getting a bit harder, and the tutor may be getting a bit tougher as assessment targets become more important. They may now be feeling:

Fed-up

The work's getting harder – and slower. The novelty's worn off. The path ahead seems like work, and *more work*.

Intimidated

The material's getting harder. The assignments are getting tougher. The marks may be getting lower. How is everyone else getting on?

Pressurized

The pace may be getting more 'forced'. Whatever happened to that 'freedom of pace' which was supposed to be the essence of open learning? But there's an exam coming up in four months . . .

Alone

Many learners may be feeling isolated – wondering if everyone else is having the same doubts, fears and even triumphs. It is very different from the class situation, where people so readily share their feelings and hopes. One of the biggest benefits of summer schools (as used in Britain, for example, in the Open University's foundation courses) is that learners quickly realize that they share many common problems, fears and hopes. Getting rid of that feeling of isolation can be a major boost to their morale.

Should I really have started this?

Life goes on. Other pressures – domestic, social, job – may all seem to be greater than ever. It's all too easy to give in and say 'I really haven't time to do all this learning as well.'

Again, of course, if learners have an open relationship with tutors, these feelings can be dealt with appropriately as and when they arise.

Learners' needs towards the end of the course

This is the time when they may well get frightened of forthcoming exams or assessments. They may need study-skills advice relating to revision strategies and exam technique. It may be many years since they prepared for an exam. For some their last experience with exams may have been disastrous.

They may be unsure about what to do next. They may need your help in sorting out the options they have for further studies. Many open learners (despite any traumas!) become addicted to open learning – it becomes a valued part of their lives. They want to continue, and they want you to advise them what they can do next. Once again, let's summarize their feelings.

Frightened

Exams do this to people. Didn't it happen to you, years back?

Will I manage it?

They can become doubtful of their ability to overcome the next hurdles. 'What will people think of me if after all this time I don't succeed?'

Why should I bother?

The original aims of studying may not be so clear now. However, some good advice about what they can do after finishing the present course can provide useful motivation.

Time seems to be rushing by!

The exam date seems to get nearer so fast!

What will life be like without open learning?

Open learning becomes addictive to many learners. Towards the end of a programme of study, they may have got so comfortable with making learning a normal part of their lives that the thought of it all ending can be very depressing.

You don't have to be face-to-face with learners to find out about these kinds of feelings. In fact the short notes learners enclose with their assignments are often quite revealing about their worries towards the end of their studies. Of course, when you have a good relationship with your learners, there's no harm asking directly: 'How are you feeling about it all now?'

Why concentrate on the negative feelings?

There will indeed be learners who suffer few if any of the negative feelings I've been listing. Your learners will include high-fliers who hardly seem to need your support at all. The high-fliers are a delight to work with – they may have bad moments but are more likely to be better able to fend for themselves. Most open learning tutors find that out of every 20 open learners they support, they will spend half their time and energy on two.

Most of your energies and skills as a tutor are needed for those learners going through bad patches or problems, which is why I have gone into so much detail about how open learners feel. Being able to help learners with difficulties has many rewards. One of these is that it keeps your dropout rate down. Your effectiveness as a tutor may be judged by some according to the dropout rate among your learners. Dropouts may not be your fault, but they might be *seen* to be your fault.

How can a good tutor help?

Set out in the following checklist are the sorts of help a tutor can give to learners as they work through an open learning programme:

■ make learners feel at ease; be friendly
■ build learners' confidence
■ help learners to feel they're not alone
■ convince learners that their worries are common ones
■ remind learners that you're there to help, not just to assess
■ reassure learners that most people make the mistakes they make
■ open up channels of communication: first name, address, telephone numbers and so on
■ take in what learners say to you in writing or on the phone; this takes conscious effort – it's easier to talk (or write) than to listen!
■ give study skills advice (but make sure it is suggestions rather than commands); help your learners to start out on their studies in an organized productive way
■ remind learners that even the hardest things can be mastered one step at a time
■ bolster your learners' egos when it comes to preparing for exams: confidence may be as important as ability
■ give practical advice regarding revision strategies and exam technique
■ remind learners that their present studies can lead them to choices and opportunities in the future
■ keep finding out what your learners would like you to do.

One good way of finding out what your learners expect of you is to ask them to tell you what they would like you to do under each of three headings: 'stop' 'start' and 'continue'. It sometimes comes as a surprise when they tell you what they would like you to stop doing – but it's well worth trying to do so if humanly possible. You may even be told 'stop being so encouraging, and give me some real critical feedback'. Fair enough if that's what they really want. The 'start' category can cover things you may never have thought of, for example 'start being more fussy about my spelling'. The 'continue' category is the good news – it's comforting to have learners ask you to continue what you've been trying to do; it's proof that you have been succeeding.

Any good tutor will try to respond to all the problems and needs we have described. How you do this will depend on your circumstances. Of the three principal possibilities – in writing, by phone or face-to-face – only one or two may be available to you. Let's look at each one separately.

Written communication

This is the most common and probably the most important means of communication between tutors and learners. There are two main kinds of written communication:

- written comments on marked work
- letters to learners, sent with marked work.

Comments written into learners' work

First, what colour should you use? Red? Green? Pencil? Think what you'd feel like if you wrote something, were proud of it, then got it back scrawled all over in red ink. Even if all the comments turned out to be congratulatory, the first sight of all that red would be demoralizing. If many of the comments were critical ... well, need I say more?

The real purpose of comments from tutors is connected with giving learners useful feedback – a vital component for successful learning. Some learners are considerate enough to leave a wide margin, which serves as space for you to add comments and suggestions. If there's no such space available, you can write your comments on separate sheets, relating them to numbers or asterisks you slot into their work. Another way of attaching your feedback comments is to use 'Post-it' notes. Somehow, these are not such an invasion as writing comments directly onto their scripts.

It's all too easy to put ticks and crosses. Obviously, crosses can be very demotivating. But even ticks can be improved upon. Here are a few words or phrases that warm open learners hearts:

'Good point'
'I agree'
'Quite so'
'Indeed'
'You're right'
'I hadn't thought of this one'
'That's the idea'
'Spot-on!'
'That's the key one'
'I like this'
'A good example'.

It makes all the difference to learners if they can see that you have read their work carefully. Such words or phrases speak louder than ticks in this respect.

Letters to open learners

You'll probably need to write a brief letter with overall comment every time you mark an assignment. It may well be entered into a space on a form, but its purposes remain the same as a conventional letter. Why do learners need such letters? First of all, think of the feelings and emotions of the average open learner as he or she reads a letter from a tutor:

- was it good enough?
- have I made a fool of myself?
- should I carry on?
- did he/she really read my work?
- is he/she trying to help me?

I can't tell you how to write the ideal letter! A letter is something from you. I can, however, remind you of some of the things that can go wrong.

Dangers to avoid in letters

There are words and phrases which cause learners' hearts to sink. It's worth remembering that learners can be very sensitive: use certain words with great caution. One dangerous comment is: 'You've obviously put a lot of effort into this assignment'. Now this is all right if the learner *has*. But what if the learner *hasn't*? There goes the trust of the learner for the tutor!

Other comments to be avoided are: 'You have not quite grasped . . .' or 'You don't seem to have understood . . .'. What does that do for the learner's self esteem? Not a lot! None of us likes to have it implied that our understanding is at fault.

We'd much rather read something like this:

Don't worry too much about . . . Most people find this a difficult area. In fact, this topic causes more problems than most things. The textbook (or module) doesn't make it as clear as I'd like it to be. Please read the extra material I've enclosed, and do let me know if it helps or not.

More 'danger' words

Some are more obvious, such as:

failed (this is almost always a 'put down' word)
error (slip, or mistake are milder somehow)
below the required standard (formal, threatening)
re-submit ('It would be worth you having another go' is more acceptable to learners)
unsatisfactory (cold, threatening).

Of course, a balance needs to be struck between pandering to learners' feelings and being honest regarding standards. In the very first letter to a particular learner, I'd advise caution. By the fifth letter, you will probably know learners well enough to know when to call a spade a spade.

I list below some characteristics of the best written communications to open learners. If you're involved in training/supervising open learning tutors, you may find it useful to apply this as a checklist to copies of some of their letters to learners. Written feedback should be:

- friendly
- comforting regarding mistakes and problems
- helpful
- to the point
- informative
- not too critical
- not too hard
- informal
- constructive
- unambiguous
- easy to read and understand: short sentences – short words where possible
- motivating
- positive
- giving praise for things done well
- unpatronizing
- building rapport
- kindly setting standards for the future.

Written feedback should get to learners as quickly as possible. There's a lot of evidence that the value of the feedback goes down rapidly if there's much delay. Learners may have moved on to other things, and the past assignment may be regarded as 'historical' if the feedback arrives weeks later! It sounds a tall order, but you should aim to mark and return work from open learners on the same day as you receive it.

Telephone communication

The telephone has several obvious advantages over the letter. First, you can have an immediate exchange of questions and answers. Second, it is easier to come across as a friendly human being on the phone. However, it is worth thinking about how to make telephone communication as effective as possible.

Listen

It's all too easy for you to say what *you* want to at the expense of listening to find out exactly what the learner needs help with. Be sure to take time to listen. Many people (including me) will gladly admit to be somewhat 'hard of hearing'; a much more serious problem is 'being hard of *listening*'! Learners may be somewhat in awe of tutors, and on the telephone this can lead them to listen rather than talk. Tutors can feel they must fill the silence to make it more comfortable for learners, rather than leave them struggling to think of what to say. It can be a vicious circle.

It can be useful to suggest to learners that they compile lists of short questions that they'd like to put to you next time they talk on the phone.

Be prepared

It's useful to have your learners' records within reach. It can make all the difference if you can readily pull out a form or card with all the important information readily to hand. That's so much better than having to ask:

Who are you again please?
Sorry, but which module are you having problems with?
What was the last work you sent me?
What grade did I give you?
Is it you that has had a new arrival in the household?
Was it you that was having trouble with . . . ?

Your records should have little notes about all sorts of things beside assignments, dates, grades and names. It's also well worth keeping up to date with other snippets of news you may receive in letters from learners, such as moving house, the antics of their children, pets, families and so on. 'How's Maggie doing with her preparation for A-levels?' is the sort of comment that shows learners you're human and that you care.

Be available

I don't mean 24 hours a day, seven days a week! Let your learners know good times to ring you up. If you are caught at a bad time, 'Can I ring you back in half-an-hour?' is better than coming across disgruntled because you're in the middle of a meal.

Another way of being 'available' is to use an answering machine. This means that you don't need to answer the phone at all when you're really not ready or willing to spend time answering learners' questions. When learners know you have an answering machine, they are usually more willing to try their luck. Your outgoing message should remind them to leave their number so that you can ring them back. Some learners even *prefer* to speak to an answering machine, and will quite happily summarize their problem into it. This gives you the chance to sort out what you're going to say in reply, and get back to them.

Make it worthwhile being phoned

Naturally, any good tutor will answer the main question that a learner telephones about. It's better still, however, to give learners who ring you up that little bit extra. Let them go away with the feeling that it was well worth ringing you up. This may lead to some extra phone calls for you, but it can help you to open up to your learners. After all, their success is your primary concern.

Don't waffle

Tempting as it is, if your learner asks you something you don't know, don't try to pretend you do. Your learner will respect you all the more for saying 'Sorry, I don't know – but I'll make it my business to find out, and get back to you.'

Don't 'stick to your agenda'

Here, I'm thinking mainly of occasions when you telephone a learner for a particular reason. It's all too easy for you to stick to that reason, when there may be other important things to deal with. It all goes back to the start of this list – being prepared to listen.

Face-to-face sessions

Some open learning schemes such as the Open University in Britain allow tutors and learners to meet. This has particular advantages in that learners can talk things over with each other and overcome the isolation felt by many such learners. The biggest danger with a face-to-face session is that the tutor comes prepared to *give* and not to *receive*. Conscientious tutors plan things to do at a face-to-face session – whether with individual learners or with a group. But over-preparation can result in tutors sticking too closely to their plans and becoming impatient when anyone asks questions that take them off course. Many of the things I suggested regarding written communication and telephone communication extend to face-to-face sessions. Here are a few more ideas.

If you've got a face-to-face tutorial session with a group of learners, get them *all* involved. There are all sorts of ways of doing this, all of which depend on breaking down formality and allowing even the shyest in the group not to feel threatened or pressurized. It helps a lot to sit your learners in a circle rather than in rows. That stops people at the back being excluded or cut off. If everyone in the group can see each other's facial expression, the group soon becomes more relaxed.

If you're doing some 'input' now and then (for example, at a blackboard or screen), you may need a U-shape rather than a circle, but try to avoid rows. In any face-to-face session, it's best to regard the *processes* as much more important than the content. I'm thinking of processes such as questioning, discussing, sharing ideas, solving problems and so on. All of these contribute to the learning process. If you were merely to provide a long lecture, there's no guarantee that much learning would occur. Think back to how boring many of the lectures you attended were! All the things mentioned above regarding written and telephone communication apply also to face-to-face sessions.

Some learners may be quite shy in face-to-face sessions. If you ask the whole group a question, it tends to be the same one or two voices that reply. Obviously, it would be very uncomfortable for the shyest learners if you were to force them to give their views when you ask a question, for example by pointing towards them or calling out their names. An easy way out of this is to use 'Post-it' brainstorm sessions in the group. Give everyone a Post-it, pose your question, then ask everyone to write down their individual answers, views or replies on their Post-it slips. This can be done anonymously. Then, allow learners to stick their Post-its on a wall or door, and let them look at what each other wrote too. This method of 'joining in' is much kinder to shy learners, and allows them to contribute equally. In fact, their contributions are often better than those from the one or two learners who would have answered all your questions orally.

Conclusions

Good tutoring all comes back to thinking of each learner as a fellow human being. You should do everything you can to open up communication so that it isn't all one-way. Listening to learners and reading their work (including between the lines) are perhaps more important skills than writing or speaking if you're going to be seen by your learners as someone who gives positive support and help. If your learners still send you Christmas cards years after their studies are over, you can regard yourself as a successful tutor.

Chapter 9

Mentor Support in Open Learning

Abstract

The last chapter explored how open learners may benefit from supportive tutoring. This chapter widens the discussion of support to that which can be given by 'mentors'. This kind of support can be formally built-in to the design of open learning schemes, or can be arranged on an *ad hoc* basis by learners (or by their supervisors or managers).

Objectives

When you've explored this chapter you should be able to:

- explain what mentoring is
- list several types of people who can be mentors
- explain the sort of things mentors can do for open learners
- describe various ways that mentoring can take place
- work out what training mentors may need
- decide how mentors should liaise with tutors – or it they should liaise at all.

What is mentoring?

A useful short definition of a mentor is 'a trusted colleague'. A mentor is usually someone in a neutral position in one way or another, for example someone not involved formally in assessing the work of learners but able to advise, encourage, support and generally 'oil the cogs' to assist the process of learning. Mentor support is particularly useful in open learning, where face-to-face contact with tutors or trainers may be limited or absent.

What's new about mentoring?

Nothing, really! Most people who have successfully learned things have had the benefit of people around them prodding, coaxing, supporting, encouraging. These people could be friends, family, colleagues, fellow-learners – almost anyone. The only difference, perhaps, with mentoring is that such help is formally recognized rather than serendipitous.

Why have mentoring?

People learning by open or flexible learning processes – particularly when learning on their own, and maybe at a distance – can suffer from the effects of isolation. This in turn is reflected in a lack of day-to-day feedback on their progress. They may not have anyone to talk things over with, and the 'digesting' stage in their learning can be impeded. They may not have anyone to encourage them when the going gets tough, and the 'want' to learn can diminish. The following reasons for arranging or providing mentor support add up to a convincing case for having a 'third party' involved in open learning.

- Although most learning is 'learning by doing', learners need someone to talk to about their learning, if it is not to become something rather artificial.
- Although feedback may be provided through the responses to self-assessment questions and exercises in the learning materials, such feedback is in print (or on the screen) and is not quite the same as human feedback, however skillfully the printed words are composed.
- Although human feedback may be provided by tutors, this can be seen only too easily as 'feedback from a figure of authority'. While such feedback is valuable and necessary, it is sometimes harder to take than feedback from an ordinary person.
- Responsibility for learning rests largely with open learners. The addition of someone to coax, encourage, prod and sympathize can help learners handle the responsibility for keeping their learning going.
- Mentoring is in itself a powerful personal-development process. It can help people who would not otherwise have worked together to build up useful and enduring relationships.

Who may the mentors be?

A surprising range of people can be effective mentors to open learners, depending on all sorts of circumstances surrounding the way the open learning is structured. People who can fulfil mentoring roles can include:

Fellow learners, giving mutual support and encouragement

This often happens informally anyway, when two or more learners are studying the same programmes. However, making mentoring a formal or official part of the learning scene brings considerable advantages to all involved – not least the learners doing the mentoring.

'A trusted friend or colleague', chosen by learners themselves

There are many advantages in allowing learners to choose their own mentors. For a start, they can choose people whose advice they value. They can choose people they have easy access to. Learners can choose people who know something about the situation in which they are learning.

A supervisor or manager

For open learners already in employment, there can be many advantages in involving managers or supervisors as mentors. These include the benefits of such people knowing more about what learners are trying to do, enabling them to smooth the way when possible. In addition, where managers or supervisors are closely involved with the open learning programme, learners have the additional incentive to keep at it so as not to be seen by their mentors as 'backsliding'.

Someone who has recently 'done it'

Sometimes the best people to help learners with a topic are those who have just learned it themselves. Such people remember only too well what the problems were, and how they tackled them. Someone who has recently mastered something can often explain it more effectively than someone who has known it for years. They can also illustrate that there is 'light at the end of the tunnel' when helping learners who seem quite stuck. In a company or organization, learners themselves may not know which people have recently learned the same (or similar) topics, but managers or personnel staff can often put learners in touch with such people.

A friend – or even a relative

Whether they know it or not, most people have been mentors. Recruiting a friend or relative into the role of mentor can be an interesting extension of the relationship already there. It's best for the learner to choose who to recruit of course – no one wants to have mentoring 'imposed' on them. Having chosen a friend or relative to act as a mentor, it's very useful to help them understand a little more about what mentoring actually is. They may well be very pleased to have been chosen, and provide valuable help and support.

The stranger as mentor

We've all found 'telling it all to a perfect stranger' valuable at some points in our lives. The advantages of perfect strangers are that there are no in-built expectations to live up to, and it's possible to walk away from the encounter 'unscathed', and usually in better spirits! Naturally, what may start as an encounter with a perfect stranger can turn into something quite different if both people get to know each other and meet more than once. A further advantage is that if things don't work out, the stranger can be 'dropped' – it's much less easy to 'drop' a mentor of the supervisor or manager category if things aren't working out.

The 'correspondence' mentor

This sort of mentor may be quite rare but such people do exist, and I for one am very grateful for them. Over the years I've had the good fortune to build up a shortlist of like-minded colleagues in different parts of the country (and other countries) whose opinions I trust and value. More important, these are people that I feel able to bounce 'raw' ideas on. I know that they won't reply 'rubbish', but come up instead with a list of questions and suggestions for me to explore, allowing me to find out for myself if and when it *was* 'rubbish'. This sort of mentoring can be used to support open learning too. There are some key requirements for 'correspondence' mentoring of course, one of which is 'a reply to anything within a couple of days' (even if only to say 'I have not time to reply in detail until next Saturday, but bear with me').

What can mentors do?

In essence, mentoring is about supporting learners, encouraging them, helping them to keep going and helping them to deal with obstacles or problems. Mentors may serve learners well by doing a selection of the things listed below (though don't imagine a single mentor doing all of these at the same time):

- simply being available for a chat, face-to-face or on the telephone
- smiling, encouraging, being optimistic about the learning programme
- helping learners feel good about what they have already achieved
- helping learners keep to deadlines and schedules: the simple fact that someone may ask you 'Are you going to have that assignment ready by next Friday?' is a powerful incentive *not* to be in the position of saying 'I'm afraid not!'
- helping learners with bits of the learning programme that have temporarily stopped them in their tracks
- 'knowing someone who can' when they can't offer direct help themselves
- helping learners plan their work, for example agreeing targets and deadlines
- giving learners informal feedback on work they do as they learn; feedback from mentors may not be as authoritative as that from tutors, but it provides a useful 'first reaction' to learners' work
- helping learners to get the most out of tutor-feedback and advice, for example encouraging them to make lists of questions they would like answered by 'an expert'
- making learning 'more possible', for example by providing time, space and facilities which learners may need to do some of their learning at the workplace

- asking simply 'How's it going?': the fact that someone will ask this is a powerful motivator since learners don't want to have to reply 'Well, nothing much is happening at present'
- helping learners 'maintain their want'; when learners are going through a difficult part of their programme, mentors can gently remind them of the value of the final goals, that tough parts are only to be expected, and that 'a problem is only a problem until you know how to solve it' and so on
- cultivating learners' feelings: 'Go on – you can do it', 'You're not on your own', 'There's someone rooting for you'.

How can mentoring be structured?

There are many different ways that mentoring can be incorporated into support mechanisms for learners. Which is most appropriate depends on the nature of the learning programme and the types of people who are mentors and learners. Below are some of the possibilities.

Timetabled mentoring

Here, mentors and learners arrange specific time slots for meetings, for example every week, fortnight or month. This sort of mentoring has the advantage of being a spur for learners, who will wish to have something to report at each meeting. Also, mentors themselves may take their role more seriously if they have it built into their own schedules, and will be likely to follow up matters arising from one meeting to the next. It's useful if 'minutes' are recorded of each meeting, for example a short summary of the matters discussed, actions agreed and interim deadlines for next steps. The notes can be made by either party, and copied to the other.

'Corridor' mentoring

This is the term I use to describe the very informal sort of mentoring which can be based on frequent meetings such as in corridors, staff rooms and canteens. This sort of mentoring works well where learners and mentors would be meeting often anyway. Most of the meetings would not be directly concerned with the mentoring process – normal workplace or social meetings in other words, but the mentoring role can gradually be built-in through this sort of informal meeting. Even when mentors and learners meet informally frequently, they often find it useful to plan a more formal 'timetabled' meeting from time to time to address any important matters arising.

'Mutual' mentoring

This is how I describe self-help pairs or small groups of learners who support each other in their learning. In colleges, such groups may work as 'study syndicates' where two or more like-minded learners meet with the express purpose of helping each other learn and solving problems that any member of the group has at a given time. The learners may not be studying exactly the same topics or programmes but they can still give each other very useful help, encouragement and support. Simply having someone willing to listen to problems is a boon. Once learners have overcome any feeling that they have to compete with each other, they can get the most out of using each other as a powerful aid to their learning.

Telephone mentoring

Mentors don't necessarily have to meet learners face-to-face every time. A quick, encouraging telephone call can make a lot of difference to learners who are going through a difficult part of their programmes. Telephone calls can be squeezed into busy diaries, and this sort of mentoring can work particularly well for professional people who are studying by open learning but who still benefit from some support or coaxing. Telephone mentoring is best, however, as a supplement to occasional face-to-face meetings.

Mentor training

When mentoring is going to be a formal component of learning programmes a 'pool' of mentors is needed at the outset. It is wise to provide one or two mentor training workshops to alert would-be mentors to the nature of the role, and to allow them to judge whether they will be comfortable in the role. Such workshops can usefully employ some role-play scenarios of learners with particular needs for support, and allow individuals or groups to suggest ways of helping with the problems. It is also useful for such workshops to address the questions on which this chapter is based, starting with 'What is mentoring?' (Indeed, this chapter grew from my experience of leading mentor training workshops.)

Learning agreements

Especially when learners and mentors start out rather unsure about how mentoring can best be developed, it is useful for them to draw up an informal 'learning agreement'. This can include what they will expect from each other and what they will undertake to do for each other. It's useful too for the learning agreement to include links to the learners' programmes of study, for example a list of target learning outcomes and target dates by which it is planned to achieve the outcomes. Such agreements are sometimes called 'learning contracts' but I think this term may be over-formal for what is ostensibly a flexible support process. It may be wise to adjust the learning agreement quite frequently as new problems emerge and old ones are overcome.

Tutoring and mentoring

In many ways, the roles of tutors and mentors overlap. Both need to be positive, encouraging and supportive. The main difference in the respective roles is that tutors are normally expected to be 'subject experts' in the topics being learned, while mentors do not need any such expertise. Also, tutors may be formally involved in assessing learners' work, whereas mentors rarely become involved in this way.

We've already looked in some detail at desirable characteristics of tutor--learner and mentor–learner relationships. It is possible for tutors and mentors to liaise too. However, if learners were to feel that mentors were conspiring with tutors behind the scenes, the vital trust needed in the learner–mentor relationship would become threatened. So, if mentors are going to liaise directly with tutors, it must be done with the full knowledge and backing of the learners themselves. That said, there are many ways that liaison between mentors and tutors can benefit learners, such as:

- mentors can liaise with tutors on behalf of learners, for example to arrange practical support at the workplace, or to explain the exact expectations of learners from their managers or supervisors
- mentors can often tell early on when learners are struggling with particular parts of a programme, and can liaise with tutors to discuss extra sources of help or information which learners could benefit from
- if a formal tutor-marked assignment is late for a good reason, a mentor can offer to authenticate the cause of the delay.

Conclusions

Despite the image of open learning being done on one's own, human support is important. The nature of many open learning programmes demands that support from human tutors, though vital in many ways, is not always available and cannot cover all needs. Mentors can bridge the gap. In practice, mentors can be even more valuable than tutors. Not least among the benefits of mentoring is the amount the mentors themselves learn – both from being involved in the processes, and also from discussing with learners the topics being studied. Mentoring has been found to be one of the most profitable of the various staff-development activities in my own institution.

Chapter 10

Open Learning in Traditional Courses

Abstract

The principles and practices of open learning are increasingly being used to bring increased variety and flexibility into traditional education and training programmes. In the first part of this chapter, I outline the sorts of situations best suited to the introduction of flexible learning components in traditional courses. The remainder of this chapter is about extending the main principles and practices of open learning to the lecture theatre. In particular, I'm thinking of lectures to fairly large groups of learners such as are given in most colleges. Many college lecturers who've become involved in open learning (as writers or tutors, for example) report that they soon begin to approach lectures quite differently. I suggest some ideas for bringing some open learning processes into the lecture room – even when large groups of learners are sitting there in rows.

Objectives

When you've explored this chapter you should be able to:

- come up with some ideas regarding how open learning may fit in with 'conventional' courses
- select the most appropriate topic areas for open learning
- describe the behaviour of learners in lecture sessions
- analyse learner behaviour in terms of activity or passivity
- list some of the problems of lectures
- outline some advantages and disadvantages of issuing handouts in lecture
- describe how handouts can be made interactive
- design interactive handout material of your own.

Mix and match

Self-study modules are the bread and butter of open learning programmes, but they can also be used to replace selected parts of conventional face-to-fac courses, such as those run in colleges and training centres. Certain parts of the curriculum lend themselves best to translation to open learning form. It obviously takes time and energy to compose such open learning modules, though it may often be possible to adapt existing published materials for such purposes. Where open learning material is being used to back up formal tuition, the quality of the modules doesn't need to aim for absolute perfection since the trainer or lecturer is still available to bridge gaps and help with problems. Even quite small elements of a course may be independently turned into open learning components – maybe in the form of handouts of no more than half a dozen pages or so. Certain hallmarks of open learning need to remain, however, to ensure effective learning:

- clear details of intended learning outcomes
- plenty of activity
- self-assessment questions and feedback
- useful summaries.

Even the smallest open learning modules benefit from the use of white space for learners to write in as they study. The white space makes the module far more compelling' – it is not just an ordinary handout, destined for filing! The justification for the extra costs (financial or in terms of time writing modules) needs to be in terms of more effective learning, and the ultimate easing of the pressure on the teacher's time. There are several particular instances where it can be well worth the time or expense to add open learning components to face-to-face courses. I will describe some of these briefly under the following headings:

- introductory material
- much-repeated lectures
- remedial lectures
- background material
- 'need-to-know-before' material
- bits you don't like teaching
- 'nice-to-know' versus 'need-to-know' material.

Introductory material

At the start of most courses, whether in training or education, the first few sessions are taken up with going over various things that the learners should know already. This is necessary to 'level' the knowledge base of the group in readiness for progress to more demanding material. However, all too often, many of the group do not in fact already know the basic material. They may well have *studied* it before – even to the level of exam success – but how much of it do they remember months (or even years) later when starting their new courses?

So, in the first few sessions, a class may consist of a diverse mixture of learners. There are those who actually know the basic material very well (and easily become bored and switched off). There are those who know very little of the basic material already (who may find the lecturer's pace too fast). The obvious solution is to provide learner-paced learning – self-study or open learning. An open learning module can be issued *instead* of the first few sessions. Learners could be briefed along the following lines:

> Come back in three weeks' time, having worked through the module I've given you. You'll need to make sure that you can achieve all the objectives in the module by then. The best way of doing this is by completing all the various activities in the module. It doesn't matter if it takes you two hours or two days – the main thing is that when you've completed the module you'll be exactly ready for our next session together.

The slower learners can spend a bit of extra time getting to the starting point for the sessions to come. The fast learners (or those who know a lot already) can skim quickly through the open learning module, slowing down only when (or if) they come to something new to them. An additional advantage of using open learning modules for going over fundamentals underpinning a course is that, when exams approach, such modules make ideal revision tools.

Much-repeated lectures

I'm thinking here about college-based courses where there may be some lectures common to a number of different classes or programmes, or overlapping areas of training programmes where the same topic seems to be needed time and again by different groups of trainees. Have you got some lectures you always seem to be giving? It can get a bit boring giving the same lecture time and time again. If it gets boring to *you*, what may be happening to it as far as your learners are concerned?

If the total numbers of learners involved are quite large, it may well be worth the time and effort needed to turn such lectures into open learning components of their courses. A much-repeated lecture is usually an important one anyway, so it is obviously useful for learners to have a ready-to-use revision aid for such parts of their courses. I'm not suggesting completely abandoning the face-to-face session, however. If the module is issued a little in advance of the lecture session, the live event can be used for discussion and questions rather than merely note taking by learners.

Remedial lectures

Even well into a course, it is often found that a significant proportion of a learner group has difficulty with some important aspect of the course. For example many engineering lecturers find that learners are still lacking in essential mathematical skills. The problem can of course be overcome by slotting in a remedial lecture now and then but this leaves less time for the central subject material. Besides, not every learner will need the remedial lectures – for the more able they'll be boring or even alienating. If the problem is anticipated, open learning modules covering the remedial material can be issued to all learners in advance of the point where they need to have mastered the material involved. Even the slower learners then have the chance to practise and develop the skills concerned before they are needed in the context of the main subject.

Remedial help is usually most needed for the sort of topics that are hard to grasp first time round. It can be helpful to preface this sort of open learning module with a 'diagnostic test' – a non-threatening one of course. This can help learners to decide whether they need to work through the module or not. For learners who really do need the module, it is a permanent revision aid ideal for such material.

Background material

I'm not thinking of the same thing as I described under 'Introductory material' earlier, though there is some overlap. More particularly, I'm thinking of those times when learners need to explore a topic *before* lectures focus on the principal concepts or facts involved. Indeed, open learning modules are *not* the best way to cover wide-ranging background material – the modules would take too long to prepare and use. However, there are still ways of assisting learners to cover the necessary background work in open learning mode. A 'study guide' can be designed to channel their background preparation along productive lines. Such a guide can refer to various sources, but at the same time it can be an *active* resource. It can use those mainstays of open learning: objectives, self-assessment questions and responses. Learners are then in a much better position to *measure* the success of their background preparation.

'Need-to-know-before' material

I'm thinking here particularly of laboratory and practical work. There is often a considerable delay before learners can be let loose on practical work – they need to have sufficient theory under their belts to make sense of it. This delay can result in unused laboratories and workshops for the first few weeks of a course or training programme, then hectic scheduling as all the learners come 'on-line' for practical work at once.

Suppose for the sake of argument that a class of 30 needed to prepare to be ready to embark on a set of five practical assignments at the first practical session. Suppose there were five short open learning modules available, each of which would give learners all they needed to be ready to start *one* of the five assignments. Better still, suppose learners were given a timetable showing which assignment they would do first and so on during the first five practical sessions. Practical work could then be started much earlier. This would avoid the long, boring (from the learners' point of view) run-up where seemingly endless theory is being presented before the relief of practical work.

Bits you don't like teaching

If you're a teacher or trainer, and if you're in a position of seniority, you can probably delegate such topics to someone else! If not, you're lumbered with them. Or are we really saying your learners are lumbered with you doing something you don't like? This may not be the most honourable reason for spending some time and energy – once – and making an open learning module out of your non-favourite topics! But who will suffer?

'Nice-to-know' versus 'need-to-know' material

A formal lecture course may well need to concentrate on the 'need-to-know' material. However, some of the 'nice-to-know' material may be quite useful for your learners, so that they gain a fuller perspective of their subject materials. The problem is simple: there's always so much more 'nice-to-know' stuff than there is time to cover it. Reference to textbooks and journals may not help the average learner since often only the highly conscientious ones follow up the references in any case. However, if the learners' task can be a little more structured, they may take it more seriously. I'm suggesting the use of structured study-guide material, with in-built activities, objectives, and even self-assessed tests. A small duplicated 'workbook', full of white space for learners to record things in as they follow up references, is much more compelling and involving than a mere list of suggested reading. How many people actually follow-up 'suggested reading' lists anyway?

Which learners are particularly helped?

Let's look at those learners in traditional training or education programmes, who can benefit most from the use of open learning modules as a natural part of their programmes.

High-fliers

These benefit by being able to work at their own faster pace through open learning components of their courses. This is better than the situation they face in lectures, where they often get bored and frustrated with the slower pace needed by many of their colleagues.

Low-fliers

These learners benefit by being able to spend the extra time they need while working through open learning modules. They are then able to bring themselves up to the same level as the rest of their group for the start of further parts of their studies. Low-fliers may need to work through modules more than once – far easier than needing a repeat of a lecture! Low-fliers can put in that extra bit of effort without embarrassment – since no one need know that they've spent extra time. Of course, effort pays dividends – open learning modules can allow low-fliers to become higher-fliers!

Absent learners

People who miss lectures or face-to-face training sessions through sickness or other circumstances may find it difficult or impossible to catch up. Copying down a colleague's notes is a poor substitute for being present at the time. Where an open learning module is being used, it is perfectly possible to catch up on it later.

Learners weak in language skills

Here I'm particularly thinking of people learning in a second language. In lectures, such learners may be spending much of their energy making sense of the words themselves, with little energy left to begin making sense of the ideas and concepts being taught. Self-study modules allow such learners the extra time they need to master the meaning of words – they can use dictionaries at will. The same applies to some areas of mathematics and engineering, which can seem like a foreign language to learners meeting concepts for the first time.

Turned-off learners

The people I'm thinking about are those who simply don't like being on the receiving end of formal teaching. Sometimes, mature learners are prone to being turned off by the formal teaching–learning situation. They may feel out of place, or they may feel that their experience is being undervalued. There are no such feelings attached to working through a good open learning module. Learners' self-esteem is maintained or increased as they work on their own.

Over-anxious learners

These are the learners who are most hurt by being *seen* to have got something wrong – for example, when giving a wrong reply to a question posed to them during a lecture. With an open learning module, they can make mistakes in private. There's less loss of self-esteem when no one else knows your mistakes. Over-anxious learners are often the ones who take revision very seriously, and they are further helped by the fact that it's much easier to revise from an active open learning module than from a mere transcript of what occurred in a lecture.

Learners with short concentration spans

In colleges, lectures tend to last nearly an hour. Left to themselves, some lecturers can happily lecture for two or three hours. On the receiving end, however, stiffness, aching muscles, 'pins and needles' and so on quickly remind us that it's not really natural to sit still for a solid hour or more. Our brains, moreover, tire rather faster than our bodies in lectures! Most people admit that even in interesting lecture-type situations, their minds wander many times. Open learning modules are a remedy for this. It's all right for one's mind to wander when working through a module. If we miss something important (and if it's a good module) we'll find out about it quite soon when we can't get the right answer in a self-assessment question, for example.

As you've seen, most learners on traditional programmes can benefit from the use of open learning components at one time or another. It may be quite impossible to introduce a wide range of open learning resource materials overnight, but the range of such materials can be gradually built up until a course contains the most suitable mix of face-to-face and open learning. The main thing is to save human skills for things that really need human skills, and to use open learning for topics where learners can benefit from working at their own pace and in their own way.

Open learning *in* the lecture situation

For the remainder of this chapter, I'd like you to think back to when you were 'at the receiving end' in traditional lecture sessions, whether in education or training programmes. First, if you *give* lectures, I'd like you to answer a few questions. (If you don't give lectures, please think about how you'd answer these questions given your past experiences in lecture rooms or classrooms.) Please be honest! Later in this chapter, I'll deal with some typical answers to these questions, and you can compare yours with these. Please don't read ahead yet!

ACTIVITY

1   What do your learners actually do for most of the time they spend in your lectures? (I didn't ask 'What would you like them to do?') Jot down a few verbs.

2   How much are your learners learning during your lectures? Go back through your answer to question 1 and decide which of the processes were active and which were passive in terms of actual learning during the lectures.

Active processes   *Not-so-active processes*

---

3   List three (or more) problems with the lecture situation. You can choose to
    list problems your learners find with the lecture situation, or problems you
    find with it.

    ■
    ■
    ■
    ■
    ■

4   List some advantages of using handout material in lectures.

5   List any disadvantages of using handout material in lectures.

Lectures: content versus processes?

The traditional lecture tends to be dominated by the content. We feel
comfortable if we have prepared the content. We feel relaxed if we know exactly
what we are going to cover in a given lecture. We feel pleased with ourselves if
we have mapped out the content for a forthcoming set of lectures.

But what about the 'processes'? There are two kinds of process to be
considered: learning processes and teaching processes. Notice I put learning
processes first. How much do our learners learn during our lectures? Do they
learn everything we cover? Think back. How much did you learn during
lectures? Did most of your real learning in fact take place *after* the lectures? You
may have used the notes you took out of the lecture room, but how often did you
more or less start from scratch regarding the real learning?

Another way of looking at the traditional lecture is the 'transmit–receive'
model: the lecturer transmits, the learners receive. But how good a transmitter
is the average lecturer? Even the best transmitters are not always on peak form!
More important, how good are learners at receiving? Does 'interference' often
interrupt reception? Interference such as (please forgive the reference to
electrical subjects here – I couldn't resist it!):

■ 'resistance' – learners who are not feeling like receiving
■ 'capacitance' (lack of) – learners who are not able to receive well, because
  they're out of their depth, or just not on top form

- 'inductance' – learners who haven't been trained regarding how to get the most out of their lectures
- 'disconnection' – learners who are sitting there entirely 'switched-off'.

So why bother with lectures at all?

By now you're probably thinking that I'm totally against traditional large-group, face-to-face sessions. However, several valuable purposes can be served by such situations, for example:

- giving a large group of learners or trainees a memorable, shared experience
- whetting their appetites to learn – creating the 'want'
- actually helping learners to learn *during* lectures.

Later in this chapter we'll look at how these purposes can be achieved. For now, let's continue to define the problems. I often ask lecturers the question which I asked you to answer earlier: 'What do your learners actually *do* for most of the time they spend in your lectures?' I have had some surprising answers. Please compare your list with the one below which I have divided into active and passive behaviour.

PASSIVE	ACTIVE
Writing what you say	Asking you questions
Writing what's on the blackboard or screen	Answering your questions
Daydreaming	Asking each other questions
Listening to you	Solving problems
Fidgeting	Discussing things with neighbours
Watching you	Deciding what's important
Looking out of the window	Fault-finding, diagnosing what's wrong with some information
Doodling	Self-assessing their work
Yawning	Making decisions and judgements
Chatting about other things	Working out reasons for things

Why are some of the most common 'activities' passive?

Note that I've even suggested that writing is passive. If learners are merely copying down something they see or hear, it can indeed be quite passive for them – ask them what they remember of what they've just written if you doubt my point! I can well remember learning from lecture notes as exams loomed up: I couldn't remember a thing about the lectures, but there were my notes as proof I had actually been there! Listening can also be passive. I admit it is possible to listen actively – a music enthusiast can listen actively, for example, paying attention to the speed, balance, interpretation and virtuosity of a performance. But in any music audience, a few members may be listening actively, and all the rest will be simply 'hearing' it. Of course, hearing can be very enjoyable. But we learn much less from things we merely hear than from things we actively listen to. My point is that a lot of hearing goes on in most lectures, but not so much active listening. (And it's not easy to tell whether learners are hearing or listening – or doing neither!)

Some problems with lectures

Despite the fact that 'the lecture', in one form or another, has been a central ingredient in education and training courses for centuries, many doubt its effectiveness as a means of engendering learning. The lecture format has many real uses in the contexts of providing a large group of people with a shared experience, or a memorable insight, or a common task-briefing, but sadly lectures are used for purposes which the format does not really support. Later in this chapter I show how some of the principles of open learning can be taken into the lecture room to address many of the problems known by most learners and many lecturers. Let us survey the problems first.

Lecturers' problems

The lecturer is usually in control of the time, place, pace, style and content. But despite all this control, there can be problems.

1   It is not always easy to control the attention of the learners.
2   The focus tends to be on what the lecturer wants to say. This might be at the expense of what the learners need to know.
3   Many lecturers don't really enjoy talking to large groups. Such lecturers may be quite shy.
4   Relatively few lecturers know how good (or bad) they are at giving lectures or presentations – they've not taken the courage (and time) to get themselves on video.
5   Having a lecture to give when you're not feeling on form is a nightmare!

6   In the lecture situation, it can be very difficult to know how much of the message is getting across – learners are very skilled at looking alert and intelligent even when almost asleep.

7   When a lecture has to be repeated to different groups, it is (naturally) almost impossible to deliver exactly the same lecture each time.

8   We can all find extra information to slot into a lecture programme. New ideas seem so important that we can't resist including them, but it's very hard to work out which of the old material to drop to make room for the new.

9   Personalities come into lectures – unavoidably. If some members of a group don't take to a particular lecturer, there's not going to be much that they will derive from those lectures.

10 When learners miss a lecture, it's rarely possible for them to have an 'action replay' (though a few lecturers commit their most important performances to video, and make the tapes available for loan in a learning resources centre).

Learners' problems with lectures

1   Learners may fail to come to the lecture at all. Copying up someone else's notes is a poor substitute for being at a *good* lecture (though 'integrating' the notes of four or five fellow learners is a productive learning experience – 'digesting'!)

2   Learners can become bored or distracted by the topic or by the lecturer, and in any case concentration spans are limited.

3   Learners may take notes, but the notes may be irrelevant, incomplete or illegible. In fact, in higher education, notemaking is a skill which relatively few learners really master. There's always the tendency to *take* notes (copy down what is seen or heard) rather than *make* notes (sift and sort the information and ideas).

4   Learners may not follow up the lecture content because they're too busy sitting in other lectures. They assume that because they've captured the notes, that will be enough.

5   Many learners are not at their best during any particular lecture. They may have got out of bed the wrong side, have a hangover, not be feeling 100 per cent, be at the wrong time of the month and so on.

6   Learners may hesitate to ask questions when they can't understand something. They don't wish to be seen not knowing or not understanding. They fear they may be the only ones not to know. (Rarely the case of course.)

7   Learners may feel little sense of achievement at lectures because of the passive role often expected of them.

8   Some learners become dependent on what they're 'fed' in lectures. They believe that if they get a firm grasp on their lecture notes, that will be

enough, and maybe they do not notice or heed references to wider reading or research.

9   Learners can feel a distinct lack of 'ownership' of what they 'receive' in lectures.

10   Some learners (I am one) hate sitting still! To think, they need to move around. It's not the norm during lectures!

Handout material

Advantages of using 'straight' handout material

From what I've said above, handout material may appear to solve a lot of problems. Thinking of the 'transmit–receive' model, handouts can mean that the learners have guaranteed reception. Or is it not as simple as this? Here are some advantages of using 'straight' handout material – the equivalent of an adequate set of lecture notes:

1   Each learner gets the same set of notes.
2   Learners don't have to do so much passive writing, copying and so on.
3   There should be more time for learners to think about the content of the lecture rather than merely trying to write it all down.
4   Learners who are slow writers are less disadvantaged.
5   Learners who are weak in language skills are less disadvantaged and have more chance to think about the content.

Disadvantages of using 'straight' handout material

1   Learners may switch off, secure in the knowledge that the handout material covers all they will need to master.
2   Learners may not come at all if they know they can get copies of handout material issued.
3   The handout material may be too extensive. It's only possible to write a few pages of notes in an hour; a handout can contain a dozen or more pages of printed material, which may be too much to learn.
4   Sometimes handouts are no substitute for learners having done something themselves. This particularly applies to drawing, sketching, calculating, problem-solving, decision-making and so on.
5   There's little real sense of ownership of something issued to everyone.

Interactive materials and processes

Let's now look at how the problems of the lecture situation and the disadvantages of ordinary handout material can be tackled using interactive handout materials and interactive processes during lectures – in other words 'open learning' at fixed place and time.

What is an 'interactive handout'?

An interactive handout is more like a miniature open learning module than a set of lecture notes. It is a handout containing white space. Every now and then during a lecture, each learner uses it to *do* something. A variety of lecture activities are structured around it. Even in a large group of learners, each one works independently at times during the lecture. I have used such handouts with groups of well over a hundred learners, but most of the advantages also apply to much smaller groups as well.

Let's take for sake of argument a one-hour lecture slot. This is how I might use interactive handouts in such a lecture.

1   The handout, consisting of two to six sides of A4, is given to each learner at the start of the lecture. (Issuing them at the very start can help with punctuality problems. One can refuse to issue them to learners arriving ten minutes late! Even more dramatic, such learners can be given pages 3 to 6, but not the first couple of pages, which may have already been 'done' in the first few minutes.)

2   The handout starts with a list of intended outcomes (or objectives). These are to give the learners a clear idea of where they should be by the end of the lecture. Knowing the intended outcomes (what the learners themselves should aim to be able to do in due course) means that when learners notice information particularly relevant to an outcome, they prick up their ears. In other words, if they're 'primed' with the key questions at the start of a lecture, learners are much more likely to notice the answers as they emerge.

3   Handouts can contain multiple-choice questions now and then. When one of these is reached, each learner can be asked to decide which is the 'best' option, or the correct option, and ring it on the handout. You can then ask for a show of hands of those who chose A and so on. Each option can then be discussed, and the reasons for the 'best' option being preferred can be elaborated with the group.

4   Every now and then, the handout can be used to *elicit* information from members of the group. This can be arranged by posing questions towards the foot of a page, leaving two or three lines worth of blank space. The learners are given a minute or two to write down their own individual answers. Then the class is quizzed orally, and the correct answers sought from learners. These may already be printed in the handout, perhaps at the top of the next page. If so, learners are asked not to read ahead (you can easily spot the odd one who turns a page before time!). This procedure is the lecture-room equivalent of self-assessment questions and feedback responses.

5   Parts of the handout can be used for revision. Learners may be asked to answer one or two short questions about the earlier part of the lecture. The group is given a few minutes for each learner to have a go, then the answers are drawn from the group orally.

6   Now and then, the handout may contain space for learners to practise things. There may be problems, and spaces for answers. A graph sheet may be included for the learners to plot data. These longer activities are best saved for the last third or so of the session. The tutor can then look over learners' shoulders and help with particular problems.

7   With interactive handouts, it is relatively easy to incorporate spaces for learners to jot down the conclusions of work in informal 'buzz groups' even when learners are packed into tight rows. The task briefings are printed in the handout, three or four learners turn towards each other and address the task, and the main findings are jotted in the handout. The key findings can be drawn from a selection of groups to round-off the buzz-group episode. (If you try structured buzz-group activities in large lecture groups, you may be surprised by how productive the activities usually turn out to be, and also by the obvious enthusiasm with which learners participate.)

8   When giving learners a few minutes to do an 'individual' task in an interactive handout, there are various ways of coping with the fact that some will finish much earlier than others. My own favourite device is to slip, without comment, a 'funny' overhead onto the screen. This can serve as a 'reward' to those who have already completed the task quickly. Learners still intent on the task don't usually divert their attention to these overheads unless my attempts at humour are too successful and there is unrestrained mirth from the 'early finishers'.

9   Occasionally (but not too predictably), it's worth using part of the handout for revision of previous lectures. After the list of intended outcomes, the first page may be given over to ten minutes of questions and spaces. After the learners have attempted the questions, the correct answers can be drawn from the group. The learners can even be shown how to mark their own answers. Learners find it very useful to have this sort of accurate estimate of how well (or badly) they are doing. Any learners who have done badly still have the comfort of not having been *seen* (except by closest neighbours perhaps) to have made mistakes. Besides, making mistakes and finding them out oneself is a good way of learning.

10   Once in a while, it's worth turning the final page or so of the handout into a short test reviewing the content of the lecture just given, or the content of a few lectures. The test can be self-assessed by learners, or occasionally collected in and marked by their tutor. One can even stick a 'Post-it' slip to each handout and ask learners to do a final short activity, leaving their answers or views stuck to the wall as they leave the lecture room. Allow a good five minutes for learners to compare their views as they file out!

Learners feel that handouts containing so much of their own efforts are very much more their own than any 'straight' handouts they may have been given. Learners get the same sort of psychological ownership of their learning as occurs with good open learning materials.

Since interactive handouts (like open learning materials) contain questions and responses, when learners need to revise the material they have a ready-made 'active revision kit'. All they need to do is to work once more through the exercises and activities in the handouts, and they have in many respects 'relived' the important parts of the original lecture. This is far more productive in learning terms than merely re-reading old lecture notes.

Even in the lecture situation, with interactive handouts and interactive processes, important bits of learning are being done under the learners' own control. Learners show every sign of enjoying buzz-group activities in lectures. In telling me 'the hour passed so quickly' they're saying that other types of hour pass very slowly. I've seen learners go to considerable lengths to file and organize attractively their collections of interactive handouts, and even index them. I have yet to see an interactive handout being used as a paper aeroplane!

The art of quizzing the group

We've seen that interactive handouts promote learner involvement with learning processes. Let's now explore one aspect of the *teaching* process in which interactive handout material is useful.

Throughout this book I've concentrated on making things as comfortable as possible for the learner. This bit may not be so comfortable, but it is useful for them – and you. Do it with a smile and a twinkle in your eye to keep the atmosphere friendly.

After giving learners the chance to complete a task and write down their answers to questions, the idea is to try to get *all* of them to the point of being ready to give an oral answer when asked. It's no use saying: 'Fred, what was your answer to question 3?' – only Fred will think; the rest will have a chance to switch off.

Think about the effect of altering the process as follows.

1   Ask everybody: 'What is the answer to question 3?'
2   Pause and look around.
3   Then pounce! 'Fred?'

Even better, don't actually look at your 'victim' as you call his or her name.

What if you don't know their names?

Even with a large group, it is possible to get each member to have answers ready. If a number is pencilled on the top corner of each handout, you can pick random numbers, and ask the owner of that handout for an answer. It only takes a minute or two to number a sheaf of handouts. If the owner of a selected number tries to remain anonymous, a neighbour can usually be relied on to give him or her away. If the same number comes up again from time to time, even someone who has already answered a question isn't safe and must remain alert. Another ploy is to ask the last learner who responded to pick a number. Then it's not your fault that the onus lands on particular learners.

Interactive handouts: solving lecture problems

Let's recall many of the problems of lecture and 'straight' handout problems that I mentioned earlier in this chapter and see the solution offered by interactive handouts. I've summarized the problems in italics and the solution in ordinary print.

1   *It is very easy for learners to remain passive or switched-off for much of the time.*
    It is not at all easy if they are frequently being asked to respond, both in writing and orally. They are also making decisions for much of the time, for example: 'What is the important point I'm supposed to write in this blank space?'

2   *It is easy for the lecturer to believe that he or she is being understood, when the truth may be very different. Learners become good at looking as though they are understanding everything, especially when they are not!*
    The lecturer can measure the progress of learners from their oral responses to questions, and can look at what learners have written in their handouts in answer to questions, and so on. The lecturer can then go over things that are causing problems at the time when the 'owners' of the problems are receptive to help.

3   *In an ordinary lecture, the lecturer may not notice real difficulties being experienced by learners.*
    If few pens are in motion when learners are asked to jot something down in their handouts (for example, the answers to questions), the lecturer immediately knows learners are having difficulty. The nature of any difficulties is revealed when individual learners are asked to say what they have written in their handouts.

4   *If ordinary handout material is issued, learners often switch off secure in the knowledge that they have already got a set of notes. This happens even when the handout is not adequate as a set of notes.*
    The interactive handout is far from a complete set of notes. It *becomes* a complete set of notes by the end of the lecture. But the most important ingredient of that set of notes is the input from the individual learner. Learners quickly realize that the printed handout is not much good as it stands. They see that their task during the lecture is to turn it into something that will be useful to them during their future learning.

5   *Learners in large groups who know that ordinary handouts are regularly issued are often tempted to skip lectures because they won't be missed and they can get copies of colleagues' handouts later.*
    With interactive handouts, the important part of each lecture is what the learners *do*. A blank, empty handout is not much good, and does not help a learner catch up on a missed lecture.

6 *When learners come to revise material given in lectures, they often have to start their learning from scratch, remembering little of the actual lecture.*
My own feedback from learners who worked through interactive handouts in lectures shows that they feel that they did a lot of learning *during* the lectures. They feel that they are far from starting from scratch when they come to revise. They often admit that they are more tired after an interactive lecture, but a lot less bored!

7 *It is difficult for even the best lecturer to keep all learners in a group 'abreast' through a lecture. Some will lag behind the lecturer, others will be ahead. Concentration spans are much shorter than lecturers would like them to be.*
With interactive handouts, each individual activity takes a relatively short time. There is less chance for concentration to wane. A change can be as good as a rest!

8 *Lecturers tend to worry about their ability to deliver good performances, especially when they're off colour or preoccupied with other worries.*
An interactive handout is in effect a 'failsafe' for a lecture. Even if you're off form, it's usually possible to lead learners through the exercises and activities contained in such a handout.

9 *Lecturers don't usually know how the learning is really progressing.*
With interactive handouts, you're frequently able to gain a sense of whether or not the learners are on top of the subject matter or having difficulties. If they beaver away each time they try an activity or exercise, you can be fairly confident that they are understanding what has been covered so far.

10 *The 'quality' of teaching and training is increasingly under scrutiny. With lectures, the quality of the performance may seem to be under the spotlight.*
Interactive handouts are excellent evidence that you've put a good deal of thought into the learning that is intended to happen in lectures. The quality of your performance is less important if the quality of the learners' experience of your lectures is demonstrably good.

11 *Personality factors come into lectures.*
This can still happen when using interactive handouts of course. However, *after* the lecture, what learners go away with is in effect a miniature open learning module. Whether or not they warmed to the event itself, they can still see the value of the interaction in the handouts, not least as an indication of what they themselves may be expected to become able to do in exams or tests.

12 *It is hard – or impossible – for learners to catch up on lectures they missed.*
When learners unavoidably miss a lecture, an interactive handout can provide them with far more information about what happened at the event than can be gained from other learners' lecture notes. Interactive handouts are not just summaries of the content of a lecture, they are skeletons of *what happened* at the lecture.

13 *Learners often feel that if they've 'got the notes' they've learned the topic.*
Interactive handouts remind learners that it's not enough just to possess

some information. They need to be able to do things with the information. The activities and exercises in interactive handouts give learners a good idea of exactly what sorts of things they may in due course be expected to demonstrate their ability to do.

14 *Other lecturers often don't seem to know what is being covered by your own lectures, and vice versa.*
Interactive handouts are excellent evidence of exactly what your learners are being trained to do. Such handouts don't just include the subject matter, but demonstrate the way that learners are being helped to *use* the information they are given.

'Devil's advocate'

The interactive kind of lecture represents a big departure from the traditional public performance lecture. As few people accept changes easily, many objections have been raised to the interactive handout. I've listed a few of them here, together with my counter-argument:

1 *It takes too long to give this much thought to designing handouts.*
Yes, it takes time at first, but designing and producing handouts are essentially skills, and it becomes faster and easier with practice. Then it begins to *save* time: it is far easier to make adjustments or additions to a couple of pages of an interactive handout than it is to rewrite parts of a handout which is continual text. The blank spaces give considerable flexibility.

2 *Learners wouldn't like them.*
Learners do in fact like them, because they soon find how much more they are learning *during* lectures – and how much less they need to do after lectures to consolidate the material. They also comment that time flies in lectures when they're doing something every few minutes.

3 *It costs too much – all that extra paper, for example!*
Yes, indeed, a six-page interactive handout costs more to produce than a two-page straight handout (or no handout at all). But if interactive handouts prove to be an effective means of promoting learning (*during* lectures as well as later) surely that in itself justifies the extra cost. Besides, if interactive handout materials are produced in bulk well ahead of each lecture, it may be cheaper than notes hastily photocopied a few minutes before the lecture starts.

4 *It's closing-up learning.*
People who say this are usually implying that interactive handout material sets the agenda for each lecture too rigidly, and that chances are lost to explore topical subjects or issues arising spontaneously during lectures. But the lecturer still has control. 'Let's leave the handout for ten minutes' may even be a welcome suggestion.

From lecture notes to interactive handouts

It's not too difficult for lecturers and trainers to translate their own lecture notes into interactive handouts. This can also be a first stage of transforming lecture notes into open learning materials. The main processes involved are:

■ deleting quite a bit of the detail – detail the learners don't need to *remember*, merely talk about and *think about* during the lecture

■ adding *blank spaces* for learners to do important things with – this is very easy!

■ writing short, simple *briefings* so learners know what exactly they should with each blank space. It's better to have such briefings printed in the handout than to rely on giving them orally during lectures – there's something about a written brief which seems to make it more likely that everyone will be trying to tackle the same task

■ designing revision tasks and so on, to form parts of the learning process during the lecture

■ providing a clear set of intended learning outcomes for each lecture at the start of each handout. It's often easier to pin down the exact outcomes *after* you've mapped out what learners will be doing during the session. The outcomes can be reiterated at the end of the handout for learners to check on what they have learned.

Conclusions

Open learning is not just something that happens at a distance, or with specially designed packages. Open learning can be made part of traditional training and education courses, and indeed some of the principles of open learning can easily be brought into the most traditional teaching situation – the lecture room. If you can do all the things set out as objectives for this chapter, I'm sure your learners will be getting a lot from your lectures. You too may feel that your time in lecture rooms is being well spent. What's more, you'll have realized that lectures and open learning are not completely different things; they are both part of the same business – the facilitation of learning.

Annotated Bibliography

This is not an attempt at a complete bibliography of literature in the fields of open, flexible and distance learning – that would take another whole book! Instead, I have listed a number of books and articles which I think are useful to colleagues working in open learning authoring and tutoring. Some of the books are directly about open learning while others contain ideas and principles which are well worth translating to open learning situations.

Bloom, B S (ed) (1972) *Taxonomy of Educational Objectives, Book 1: Cognitive Domain* Longman, London

Bloom, B S Krathwohl, D R and Masia, J F (1971) *Taxonomy of Educational Objectives, Book 2: Affective Domain* Longman, London.
These references are now somewhat historical but represent a milestone in 'firming-up' the intended outcomes of education and training by writing objectives. The present-day fashion of writing competence descriptors is built on this work.

Bosworth, D P (1992) *Open Learning* Cassell, London.
An excellent review of the development of open learning in the United Kingdom in the 1980s. The book is well referenced, and promotes thinking about learner-centred approaches.

Boud, D (ed) (1988) *Developing Student Autonomy in Learning* Kogan Page, London.
Open learning necessarily involves increased student autonomy. Anyone sceptical of students' ability to develop such autonomy will find convincing evidence in this book that students are well able to take charge of many aspects of their own learning, given suitable support and guidance.

Bourner, T and Race, P (1991) *How to Win as a Part-Time Student* Kogan Page, London.
An interactive open learning book, based on research on the problems experienced by part-time and mature students.

Bourner, T and Barlow, J (1991) *The Student Induction Handbook – Practical Activities for Use with New Student Groups* Kogan Page, London.
'Induction' is something which open learners working on their own can miss out on. This book provides many ideas regarding the kinds of activities which can help learners in general to tune-in to a course of study.

Burns, H, Parlett J W and Redfield, C L (1991) *Intelligent Tutoring Systems – Evolutions in Design* Lawrence Erlbaum, New Jersey and London.
A wide-ranging examination of the support needs of learners, and ways in which these can be addressed by interactive technology.

Dean, C and Whitlock, Q (1988) *A Handbook of Computer-Based Training (2nd Edition)* Kogan Page, London.
A good lead in to the vast field of designing interactive computer software.

Ellington, H I and Lewis, A (1992) 'Converting a Conventional Taught Course into Distance Learning Form' in Saunders, D and Race, P (eds) *Developing and Measuring Competence* Kogan Page, London.
An objective discussion of how a conventional course can be transformed into an open learning one, without going to the lengths of commissioning fully-fledged stand-alone open learning materials.

Ellington, H I, Percival, F and Race, P (1993) *A Handbook of Educational Technology* Kogan Page, London.
A wide-ranging book, linking many varieties of 'educational technology' to the processes of learning. The book contains a substantial glossary of terminology (jargon!) associated with educational technology, interactive learning and computer-based training.

Ellington, H I and Race, P (1993) *Producing Teaching Materials (2nd Edition)* Kogan Page, London.
A book giving a broad discussion of the principles and practices of designing learning resources of many kinds, and of using everything from blackboards to computer conferences. A brief review of the design principles for open learning materials is included, with some examples.

Fairbairn, G J and Winch C (1991) *Reading, Writing and Reasoning – a Guide for Students* SRHE/Open University, Buckingham.
Though this book is aimed at students, many a tutor will learn a great deal from it. The principles advocated can help authors of open learning materials to get their message across clearly and interestingly.

Fletcher, S (1991) *Designing Competence-Based Training* Kogan Page, London.
Fletcher, S (1992) *NVQs, Standards and Competence* Kogan Page, London.
Fletcher, S (1992) *Competence-Based Assessment Techniques* Kogan Page, London.
A very readable selection of books, giving up-to-date information on the development of competence in vocational education and training. These books will be particularly useful for writers of open learning materials wishing to express intended learning outcomes in terms of competence statements, range statements and performance criteria.

Gibbs, G, Habeshaw, S and Habeshaw, T (1989) *53 Interesting Ways to Assess Your Students* TES, Bristol.
Though these ideas on assessment are written for consideration in the context of conventional courses and programmes, many of them provide useful food for thought about how assessment can be made more useful to open learners.

Gibbs, G and Jenkins, A (eds) *Teaching Large Classes in Higher Education* Kogan Page, London.
Open and flexible learning have a major part to play in addressing the problems caused by increasing class sizes in further and higher education. This book contains many useful ideas about the problems and possible solutions.

Hall, R M (1992) 'Using Computer Conferencing to Develop Competence' in Saunders, D and Race, P (eds) *Developing and Measuring Competence* Kogan Page, London.
Computer conferencing is in many respects closely associated with open learning; it is interactive, can be done at a pace, time and place chosen by learners, and provides interactive responses from peer-group members and tutors alike – sometimes very quickly.

Hammond, M and Collins, R (1991) *Self-Directed Learning: Critical Practice* Kogan Page, London.
A delightfully readable book, including a considerable amount of interaction. Learner autonomy is obviously central to open learning, and critical reflection is just as important.

Harrison, N (1990) *How to Design Effective Computer-Based Training. How to Design Effective Open Learning Packages* McGraw Hill, Maidenhead.
Interesting examples of interactive material, showing many of the features of good open learning resources. Perhaps rather rigid at times, however.

Jones A, Kirkup, G and Kirkwood, A (1992) *Personal Computers for Distance Education: the Study of an Educational Innovation* Paul Chapman Publishing, London.
This book is a detailed case-study of the use of personal computers in distance learning programmes run by the Open University (UK). The insight into the running of a large distance learning organization is as interesting as the detail of the introduction of personal computing.

Jaques, D (1991) *Learning in Groups (2nd Edition)* Kogan Page, London.
For too long, open learning was thought of as individualized learning. Open learning schemes can benefit greatly by providing opportunities for learners to learn in peer-group meetings, whether formal or informal. This book makes a powerful case for capturing such benefits in any sort of learning programme.

Kemp, R and Race, P (1992) *Promoting the Development of Personal and Professional Skills* CVCP Universities Staff Development Unit, Sheffield.
This is part of a series of staff development materials aimed at university lecturers. The series as a whole incorporates a certain degree of interaction, though not in the full 'self-assessment' mode. However, this particular volume contains some examples of interactive materials which aim to help learners develop various transferable skills.

Lockwood, F (1992) *Activities in Self-Instructional Text* Kogan Page, London.
A key text for anyone designing open learning materials, particularly concentrating on the design of learner activities and feedback responses.

Mager, R (1991) *Preparing Instructional Objectives (2nd Edition)* Kogan Page, London.
A very useful book for details of ways of expressing intended learning outcomes in the format of behavioural objectives.

Mast Learning Systems (1988) *Secrets of Study* Mast Learning Systems, 26 Warwick Road, London SW5 9UD.
Secrets of Study is an interactive video package on study-skills development, and is also published as a computer-based learning package. Perhaps the strongest link to open learning principles is the care taken in the programme to *respond* to the choices learners make while using the package on-screen. The package combines six study-skills modules with a spy-thriller interactive adventure; the study-skills are needed to learn some information on volcanoes, to prevent being detected while spying at a vulcanology conference!

Morgan A (1993) *Improving Your Students' Learning: Reflections on the Experience of Study* Kogan Page, London.
This book grew largely from the experiences of students studying with the Open University (UK). It is highly relevant to authors and tutors on open learning schemes, and will help them keep the quality of learning firmly on the agenda.

Newble, D and Cannon, R (1991) *A Handbook for Teachers in Universities and Colleges* Kogan Page, London.
A user-friendly book. Coverage includes the design of various sorts of learning-resource materials, and an emphasis on learning rather than teaching.

The Open Learning Directory 1992 Pergamon Open Learning, Oxford.
A massive manual giving details of a wide range of open learning materials available in the UK, with costs, prices, contact addresses and product descriptions. The directory also includes sections on delivery centres.

Osborne, C (ed) (1992) *International Yearbook of Educational and Training Technology* Kogan Page, London.
This series of yearbooks contains useful details of 'who is interested in what' worldwide, as well as names and contact addresses of various societies and professional associations relevant to open learning and educational technology.

Paul, R (1990) *Open Learning and Open Management: Leadership and Integrity in Distance Education* Kogan Page, London.
Probably the winning ingredient of this fascinating, amusing and readable book is the material on the effective management of open learning, and suggestions for moving teaching staff from traditional approaches to flexible ones.

Percival, F, Lodge, S and Saunders, D (1993) *The Simulation and Gaming Yearbook 1993* Kogan Page, London.
In the widest sense, games and simulations are highly advanced forms of flexible learning, with overt 'learning by doing', often with the particular

advantage of immediate feedback. This yearbook (the first in a projected series) is an excellent introduction to the field, and contains many fascinating ideas which will lend themselves to incorporation in open learning resource materials – particularly those expressly designed for use by groups of learners rather than by individuals.

Race, P (1989) *Teaching and Learning in Higher Education: Series 3* (a suite of nine booklets on study-skills topics) CICED Publications, Aberdeen.
This series of small booklets is flexible learning at its most basic and least expensive! The booklets were designed to be given to students in higher education rather than sold. They do, however, contain self-analysis questions, each of which has a detailed 'response' towards the end of the booklet.

Race, P (1992) *53 Interesting Ways to Write Open Learning Materials* TES, Bristol.
This volume is more of a 'how to do it' book than the present one, with an attempt to divide the main ideas into manageable chunks.

Race, P (1992) *500 Tips for Students* SCED/Blackwell, Oxford.
This is not an open learning book – in fact, it's a textbook! However, it can be said to be user-friendly, and may give some ideas on informal style to open learning authors. More importantly, it may remind designers of learning materials of what it feels like to be a learner, and some of the problems that learners encounter.

Race, P and Brown, S (1993) *500 Tips for Tutors* Kogan Page, London.
Though only mentioning open learning in brief, the themes of this book are active learning and helping college-based learners to gain control of their own learning. Both principles apply to open learning too.

Rickards, T (1992) *How to Win as a Mature Student* Kogan Page, London.
Many open learning schemes cater for mature students in particular. Authors and tutors on such schemes will find it useful to remind themselves what it feels like to be a mature student – this book gives an excellent taste.

Rogers, C (1983) *Freedom to Learn for the '80s* Merril, Columbus, Ohio.
A pioneering book on learner-centredness. Putting the principles in this book into practice in open learning systems is an important step towards creating effective resources and management systems.

Rowntree, D (1989) *Assessing Students – How Shall We Know Them? (Revised 2nd Edition)* Kogan Page, London.
This well-respected book will be of particular value to those building assessment into open learning schemes.

Rowntree, D (1992) *Exploring Open and Distance Learning* Kogan Page, London.
Indispensable for anyone interested in designing open learning materials or tutoring open learners. It is an interactive book, with 'suggested objectives' at the start of chapters, action plans, suggested follow-up activities and thorough referencing to a wide range of the literature on open learning.

Saunders, D and Race, P (eds) (1992) *Developing and Measuring Competence – Aspects of Educational and Training Technology XXV* Kogan Page, London.
A collection of conference papers on various aspects of competence, this book gives a broad picture of the various ways in which competence is being addressed in education and training.

Stephenson, J and Weil, S (eds) (1992) *Quality in Learning* Kogan Page, London.
A broad collection of articles, giving examples of attempts to improve and enhance the quality of learning in a variety of settings. Parallel considerations about the quality of the open learning experience are useful.

Steinberg, E R (1991) *Teaching Computers to Teach (2nd Edition)* Lawrence Erlbaum Associates, New Jersey and London.
A useful source for readers wishing to extend open learning principles into computer-based environments. It is a useful 'how-to' book, well illustrated with examples.

Stimson, N (1991) *How to Write and Prepare Training Materials* Kogan Page, London.
A practical, down-to-earth book on the design and use of training materials. The principles lend themselves well to the creation of effective open learning materials.

Tessmer, M and Harris, D (1992) *Analysing the Instructional Setting* Kogan Page, London.
Although not specifically about open learning, this book serves a very valuable purpose in alerting readers to the importance of the learning environment for all kinds of learning.

Thorpe, M (1988) *Evaluating Open and Distance Learning* Longman, Harlow.
An excellent starting place for those wishing to make a deep, systematic evaluation of the effectiveness of open learning resources and systems.

Walkin, L (1991) *The Assessment of Performance and Competence* Stanley Thornes, Cheltenham.
Essentially, this is a book about training, but the excellent detail about assessing competence and performance extends admirably to measuring the 'output' of open learning systems.

Weil, S W and McGill, I (eds) (1989) *Making Sense of Experiential Learning* Open University, Milton Keynes.
Open and flexible learning are necessarily 'experiential' in many respects. This book contains many useful ideas on how experiential learning relates (or fails to relate) to 'conventional' teaching and training.

Wilkin, M (ed) (1992) *Mentoring in Schools* Kogan Page, London.
Mentors are playing an increasingly important role as supporters of open learning, especially in schemes based in commerce and industry rather than in educational institutions. Although this book is not directly about open learning, it will be invaluable to anyone wishing to train mentors and introduce mentor support for open learners.

Keyword Index

Several themes run throughout this book, and it has not been attempted to index them in detail. They include:

active learning, interaction, learner-centred approaches, feedback to learners, flexible approaches, learning processes.

Meanwhile, I hope that the keywords I have listed below will help you to track down the parts of the book where particular themes or topics are introduced.